The Making of
MODERN
LONDON
1914 - 1939

The Making of MODERN LONDON 1914 ~ 1939

GAVIN WEIGHTMAN
STEVE HUMPHRIES

Sidgwick & Jackson
London

For John and Doreen Weightman
and Nan Tucker

First published in Great Britain in 1984 by
Sidgwick & Jackson Limited
Reprinted November 1984
Reprinted December 1984

The quotation on page 51 is taken from **English Journey**
by J.B. Priestley, published by William Heinemann Limited

Designed by Ray Hyden
ISBN 0-283-99105-4 (hardcover)
ISBN 0-283-99106-2 (softcover)

Typeset by Tellgate Ltd, London WC2
Printed and bound in Great Britain by
Biddles Ltd, Guildford and King's Lynn
for Sidgwick & Jackson Limited
1 Tavistock Chambers, Bloomsbury Way
London WC1A 2SG

Frontispiece: Winter Sales, a London Transport poster
by H.S. Williamson

CONTENTS

ACKNOWLEDGMENTS

We should like to thank everyone who has helped in one way or another in the making of this book. For help with information and our interpretation of inter-war London history, special thanks to Alan Jackson, and to Steve Schifferes, Theo Barker, Peter Hall, Jerry White, Oliver Green, Ken Young, Andrew Saint and Colin Sorensen. For assistance with interviewees, thanks to Noreen Branson, Colin Ward, Bob Little, Tricia Adams, Vincent Rea, Mandy Ashworth, Fiona St Aubyn, Rosetta Bain, Paul Couesland and the LWT Community Unit, all the newspapers – too numerous to mention – who published our appeals for memories, and the old people's homes and reminiscence aid groups who have helped us to locate interviewees.

For help with various aspects of our research, thanks to Dennis Hardey of Middlesex Polytechnic, Valerie Bott of the Grange Museum, Chris Ellmers of the Museum of London, Jim Hovell and David Housden of Hoover Ltd, Anthony Rau and Philip Cakebread of J. Walter Thompson Ltd, Anthony Burgess-Wise of Fords, Vick Yeats of Selfridges, the Abbey National and the Woolwich Building Societies, the London Electricity Board, Alison Stallibrass and Joan Pepper of the Pioneer Health Centre, and the London Library.

For assistance with picture research, special thanks to Philippa Lewis and also to Chris Denver of the GLC Archives Department, Dot Davies of Middlesex Polytechnic, and Phil Philo of Gunnersbury Park Museum.

Finally, thanks are due to our colleagues and friends at LWT and to everyone that we interviewed.

Photographs and illustrations were supplied or are reproduced by kind permission of the following: Abbey National Building Society, 111/1, 111/2, 128/2; Aerofilms, 55; Baxter, Payne and Lepper Ltd, 100, 113/2, 113/3; Bede Gallery, Jarrow, 50; Lydia Bonnett, 116; Charles K. Bowers and Sons, 44-5, 60, 61; BBC Hulton Picture Library, 14-15, 18, 19/1, 39/1, 96, 136, 140, 148, 155, 164, 171/1, 171/2; GLC Archives, 101, 103, 104, 105, 108, 110, 118, 138, 144-5, 166, 169; Grosvenor House Hotel, 24, 31, 32; Gunnersbury Park Museum, 57, 58, 59/1, 59/2, 62; John Harvard Local Studies Library, Southwark, 162/2; Heinz and Co. Ltd, 64; ICI, 39/2; Ideal Home, 120; Imperial Tobacco Co., 38; Imperial War Museum, 19/2; IPC, 128/1; Kensington and Chelsea Library, 28; London Electricity Board, 52, 129, 130, 131; London Transport Museum, frontispiece, 22, 65, 68, 70-1, 73, 79, 81, 82, 86/1, 86/2, 88/1, 88/2, 88/3, 90, 91/1, 91/2, 92, 93; J. Lyons and Co. Ltd, 41; Sir Robert McAlpine and Sons Ltd, 30, 47; Fred McLeod, 163; Margaret Monk, 156; National Motor Museum, 97; Joan Pepper, the Pioneer Health Centre Ltd, 161; Pictorial Press, 162/1; Selfridges, 25, 26, 27; Steve and Doris Sumner, 151, 152; Lady Strickland, 35, 43; John Topham Picture Library, 48, 76, 134, 153, 165; Lil Truphet, 124, 125; Wates Builders, 113/1, 132, 133.

INTRODUCTION

F OR THAT generation of Londoners whose memory spanned the period from the capital's Edwardian heyday to the outbreak of the Second World War in 1939, there was absolutely no doubt that their great city, the Heart of the Empire, was transformed. It had become shockingly and excitingly 'modern', pulsing to a syncopated American beat that pervaded the whole of its teeming life from the West End cocktail party to the Hollywood movie showing to packed houses in a picture palace in Tooting. Large parts of the Victorian and Georgian fabric were torn down as London was invaded by forces that gave rise to a new architecture, much of which reflected an alien culture blowing across the Atlantic from America, or emanated from the futuristic movements in Europe.

However, though the thirties have now come into vogue, and there is a kind of bitter-sweet nostalgia for the inter-war years, the drama and excitement of the period has been obscured by the very rapid change in London life since the Second World War. What was spanking new in 1930 now appears to be quaint: not quite 'historic' but decidedly out of date. The picture palace is boarded up or turned into a bingo hall; the hotel which was the last word in modernity in 1929 has been given a kind of plastic surgery in the fifties and sixties; the splendid department store has closed down; the Joe Lyons Corner House is literally a museum piece. Because it now looks forlorn, the surviving architecture of the period encourages the view that the 1920s and 1930s were years of sad decline. For inter-war London there is no royal title – Georgian, Victorian, or Edwardian – to suggest it had a style or grandeur comparable with earlier periods. This was 'the Depression' or 'the Devil's Decade'.

But how many tourists, or Londoners themselves, are aware as they walk down Regent Street that the great buildings, which form the curving canyon of the Quadrant from Piccadilly Circus to Oxford Circus, nearly all date from the 1920s? The whole of Regent Street was rebuilt from 1908 onwards, and it is only to the north, by Regent's Park, that the original architecture of John Nash survives. What is so confusing, and so easily disguises the tremendous vigour of London between the wars, is that the street pattern remained more or less the same in the centre, while the scale and rate of rebuilding was tremendous. Regent Street rebuilt follows the same route as Nash's grand avenue of the 1820s: the map of London changed hardly at all, while its fabric and social life underwent a very rapid evolution.

Once you have an eye for inter-war architecture, which is often deceptively 'classical', you begin to understand that in the inter-war years London was not the ailing capital of a declining nation: it was a boom town. Great new office blocks were built; West End squares were completely restructured; massive new hotels arose along Park Lane; and on the outskirts of the Edwardian capital, modern factories multiplied as a vast new industrial belt arose. The built-up area of Greater London actually *doubled* in this period, as semi-detached suburbia spread out over the countryside and market gardens that had ringed the Victorian city, and the population rose to over eight million from around six million in just twenty-five years.

There is no doubt that London lost between the wars something of the exciting originality it had in the nineteenth century. New York, with its Manhattan skyscraper skyline, was far more the gleaming monument to a new kind of twentieth century industrial age and grew much faster than London. But in a way it was precisely *because* London changed with the times that it was so prosperous. It was still a great capital, if not the greatest in the industrialized world, and attracted from across the Atlantic a wave of American industry, commerce and culture.

It was after the Great War that this became most noticeable in London, as the newly developed American consumer society began to take hold and the grand houses of the West End tumbled down to make way for car showrooms, apartment blocks and hotels designed with the American tourist in mind. It is understandable that many people believed that the rapid changes in London after 1918 were really a consequence of the Great War, which so weakened Britain in the world and appeared to destroy its old social fabric. Though historians still argue about the true influence of the war on British society, most accept that it was not only the cataclysmic events from 1914 to 1918 which were responsible for creating a new world. The history of London illustrates clearly how many of the changes that occurred in the inter-war years had begun to take shape before 1914, and this is true of what was known in the early 1900s as 'the American invasion'.

By the end of the nineteenth century the American economy had developed mass-production techniques, new styles of management, and giant corporations which began to engage in a kind of economic imperialism. The first really conspicuous sign that Americans were moving into Britain and Europe in the early 1900s was the great British-American tobacco war which turned out to be a dramatic example of what was to come. The American Tobacco Company bought out one small British tobacco firm and announced it would take over the whole industry. The British response was the formation of the Imperial Tobacco Company, from twenty-five smaller companies, to beat off American Tobacco. The warring giants of the industry then formed British-American Tobacco, and proceeded to carve up the world market. British-American, characteristically, built themselves a headquarters on Millbank in 1915. It was an early example of the office block invasion of central London, which took off in the twenties, and which today still gives the Embankment north of the Thames much of its character.

Culturally, too, the Americans had arrived. Ragtime music reached Britain around 1906, and Tin Pan Alley was creating perfect English songs like *Nellie Dean* or *Down at the Old Bull and Bush*: these were both written in New York.

Though the old guard of London's society was alarmed by all this, the capital as a whole profited tremendously from the American invasion. Because it was still the greatest metropolis in the Western world, London attracted the interest and money of emerging American millionaires. So, while the rest of Britain suffered a steady economic decline, as its traditional industry based on coal and steel was undermined in the second industrial revolution, London drew the new wealth to itself. In 1909, for example, Gordon H. Selfridge, with a fortune amassed in Chicago, decided to make his mark in London, opening the first stage of his jazzy new store in Oxford Street.

This is a recurring theme in the story of the growth of inter-war London, and is picked up again in the second chapter of this book, which describes the growth of new industry around the fringes of the capital after the First World War. A great Empire Exhibition held at Wembley in 1924 and 1925, for which the Stadium was built, represented in part an attempt to promote Britain's Imperial trade. In fact it did very little in that direction, but when the site was abandoned it was quickly colonized by firms moving out of the centre of London or setting up for the first time, mostly to make products for the capital's vast consumer market. Almost an industrial shanty town at first, the region stretching right round from the north-east of London to Wembley and down to Twickenham took on a kind of futuristic quality with an architectural style which only in recent years has been really appreciated. The new arterial roads, built on the fringes of the pre-1914 built-up area, became a showplace for firms like Hoover, Firestone, Gillette and Trico. American companies in particular were attracted to the Great West Road, and J.B. Priestley commented in his *English Journey* of 1934 that to drive along it was like rolling into California.

London was able to expand at this pace between the wars because of a transport revolution which was more or less complete by 1914. First, electric power had extended the speed and range of the Underground system from 1890 when the first deep-level tube was built. Steam had entirely given way to electricity by 1905, with the conversion of the Metropolitan and Metropolitan District Lines, and the building of the first section of the Central Line in 1900. And in one quite extraordinary period of the capital's transport history, American funds were brought in to build three new tube lines in 1906 and 1907.

Trams were rapidly electrified from 1901, and it seemed at that time that electric power was the thing of the future. Then the first successful motor bus arrived and was sweeping all before it when war broke out. After the war, one combine – the Underground Group – which controlled most buses, tube lines and several tram companies, set the tone and style of what was to become London Transport in 1933. The Group was headed by a man called Albert Stanley, later Lord Ashfield, who had been brought over to London from New Jersey before 1914. The Underground Group's streamlined, modern style was the creation of Frank Pick, an Englishman with a taste for European architecture.

For several years the Underground Group pursued an expansionist policy in London, pushing out new lines to Edgware, Morden and Cockfosters, and laying the framework for the most extraordinary period in the history of house-building in London. We call this *The Battle for the Suburbs*, for after 1918 there was a considerable expectation that the state would for the first time provide more housing than private enterprise as local councils began the promised 'Homes Fit for Heroes' programme. At first, the London County

Council, influenced by the Garden City Movement, built its own municipal suburbia, vast 'cottage' estates in places like Becontree, Watling and Downham. These still have a rural quality today, and are a monument to the short-lived optimism of the post-war years.

But by the mid-1920s, private house-building took off in a spectacular fashion, and in quite a new way, with the appearance on the scene of the home owner, funded by building societies whose coffers were swelled by small investors looking for a safe place for their money. In the 1930s, the competition amongst builders, the speed of building, and a fall in the cost of materials and labour drove house prices down to their lowest ever level. In an effort to sell new estates, developers indulged in a razzamatazz which seems quite extraordinary today.

The desire for a small plot in some kind of semi-rural idyll was very powerful in the years just after the Great War. A number of pioneers, too poor to buy a house in London and yet ineligible for, or unattracted by, council housing, bought plots of land on the rural fringes of the capital and built their own homes. These were the Plotlanders, who horrified the emerging professional planners by constructing houses from old railway carriages, odd bits of wood and abandoned buses in places like Essex. For many Plotlanders their little wooden shanty in the East was heaven, but it was a far cry from the new concept of an 'Ideal Home' which emerged in the inter-war years.

One of the most fascinating aspects of the 1920s and 1930s is the story of how the modern home with its modern housewife took shape. In particular, the position of women – who had shown during the war that they were quite capable of doing men's jobs and had, for those over thirty, won the vote in 1918 – was crucial. Whatever their social status, domestic chores had been women's main occupation before 1914, either as servants or as household managers. But the arrival of a host of 'labour-saving' devices, from the gas oven to the electric iron and the vacuum cleaner, promised a freedom from household drudgery. But this promise was in a way illusory, for the convention that married women should give up work on their wedding day and should become a new kind of domestic technician in the new servantless Ideal Home created a kind of professional housewife, welded to the kitchen sink. Although for the great majority of women the true social revolution did not take place until the 1950s and 1960s, for a select group of the new middle class of the thirties it was already there, complete with a range of technical household magazines, a host of which started publication in the early 1920s – among the first, *Good Housekeeping*, arriving predictably from America.

London became in a way more 'home-centred' in this period, as housing conditions improved for a great many people, and radio and the cinema – with picture palaces built out in the suburbs – provided a rival attraction to the pub and the street. But throughout the inter-war years, the new London of the semi-detached house and electronic gadgetry existed alongside a Dickensian world of the slums in the inner city. In privately rented rooms, families still cooked over coal fires and ate their meals by gas light. Not everyone could afford the escape to suburbia or to a cottage council estate. So the drive to improve the lot of poorer people continued. Immediately after the First World War, there was on the one hand a great expectation among social reformers that a new world would be built in which poverty was abolished; and on the other an unusual willingness on behalf of the government to consider dramatic social change, as revolution was in the air in Europe and Britain's citizen army had yet to be demobilized.

These expectations were to be dashed one by one, as the nationalization of railways, mines and shipbuilding, established during the war, was disbanded, and money for housing was cut back during the first economic slump in 1921. However, as the Labour Party came to power in local government in places like Poplar, so they began to build socialist states in miniature, dubbed by a largely hostile Press as 'little Moscows'. The Victorian Poor Law was still intact in the twenties, with its workhouses and harsh regime. The dockers, dustmen and the like who were elected as Poplar Poor Law Guardians, fighting to change this system, ran into conflict with the government and were jailed.

But this kind of radical reformism, initiated to a large extent by working-class people, suffered a fatal blow in 1926 when, after a turbulent period of industrial unrest, the trades unions of the Triple Alliance – miners, railwaymen and transport workers – took on the government, and lost. After that there were few attempts at radical political change. Instead, an extraordinary movement of middle-class reformers – doctors, local councillors, planners, architects – attempted to carve a new and better world out of London's old fabric.

We have called their vision *A Brave New World*, for it encompassed all the 'wonders' of modern science: the council solarium in which children, denied health-giving sun by London's smoky atmosphere, were paraded under sun-ray lamps; the new lidos in the parks with their sun-bathing areas; the swings, flowers, light and fresh air promoted by the first Labour administration of the LCC under Herbert Morrison. These were the years before the creation of the National Health Service, when individual scientists and doctors campaigned for the poor with pioneer schemes like the health centre set up in Peckham in 1924. There were similarities to the great Victorian philanthropic movement of the 1880s, but the aims were less pious; a pagan belief in sunshine rather than a determination that morality should be the saviour of the London poor.

Over the whole panorama of London life the years from 1914 to 1939 are fascinating as a transitional phase between Victorian social ideals and the modern welfare state. Government became much more involved in business, industry, health, social services, housing, and transport, but always stopped halfway to nationalization. Much of what was dazzlingly new and vigorous was actually created only because the government, in its efforts to relieve unemployment, underwrote the capital cost of private industry. The new tube lines to Edgware or Stanmore, even the rebuilding of Piccadilly Circus Underground Station, were the product of such unemployment schemes, as were the new arterial roads, along which the middle-class car owners might motor to visit a mock-Tudor road house, all the rage in the thirties.

It was war, once again, that ended the era. Semi-detached houses were being offered for sale with bomb shelters by 1938, and Londoners were issued with gas-masks. The fear of enemy bombardment in the impending conflict was taken seriously: terrifying estimates of how many Londoners would die in air raids were issued. The enormous concentration of resources in the capital now appeared to be a terrible strategic error, and plans were made to decentralize. It was the beginning of the end of the great expansion of London.

In the year before war broke out, there was a sudden nostalgia for the Victorian past, the old London which the inter-war years had done so much to remove and improve. A song and dance routine from a show called 'Me and My Girl' swept right across the capital, a celebration of a Victorian working-class street performed in the West End and East End alike. This was *The Lambeth Walk*, which captured the world's imagination – Mussolini is said to have ordered a pretty lady over to Milan to teach it to him. It was London's swansong as the greatest metropolis in the Western World.

CHAPTER ONE

THE INVASION OF LONDON

W HEN WAR was declared on Germany in 1914, the great edifice of Victorian and Edwardian London ceased to expand after more than a century of phenomenal growth. The nation's wealth and energy were rapidly consumed by the war effort; the capital's physical fabric froze like a modern Pompeii, while its social life underwent a revolution. Liveried footmen, who not long before had served cakes to young ladies in grand houses of the West End, were in the trenches. Women domestics exchanged their frilly aprons for overalls and were fitting detonators into the nozzles of shells. Wealthy young men who had paraded in Hyde Park during the London Season were recuperating there now in bath chairs or hobbling around on crutches. Their lady friends ran canteens for munitions workers, nursed wounded soldiers, took office jobs in the City and the Ministry of Munitions, ate out alone at night unchaperoned, and smoked cigarettes in public. Bankers, solicitors and accountants, too old to fight, doffed their daytime dress and donned blue uniforms to man the searchlights for London's air defences, and were amused to find they were mistaken in this unfamiliar attire for porters on the Underground.

It was as if the old London had been reinhabited by a quite different people. And when the war was over, and London's great economic machine began to work again, it seemed to many contemporary observers that a race had disappeared: Victorian attitudes and values had died in the trenches and the great domestic upheaval of the war years. Nearly all of London's physical fabric was still there, intact: the great houses of Park Lane, Mayfair and Belgravia; the solemn edifices of the City of London's great counting houses; the canyon-like dockland and miserable workshops of the East End; and all those miles of nineteenth-century terraces and semi-detached 'villas' built to house London's vast, servant-employing middle class in modest, antiquated comfort.

But the world which built that immense metropolis had come to an end, and when, very soon, London began to expand again beyond its pre-war frontiers it took on a quite unfamiliar appearance. No more Kensingtons, Claphams or Islingtons, with their serried ranks of terraced houses, ornate churches and railway stations were created. Instead, there were gnomish rows of semi-detached houses with their miniature shopping parades, and jazzy new factories built along expanses of 'arterial' road. By 1939, when war once again put an end to the outward growth of the capital, this new, semi-detached London completely surrounded the old capital like the encampment of a foreign power. It was as if London had been invaded by an alien culture, and the same forces which had given rise to semi-detached London had swept through the old Heart of the Empire and given it a zest and glitter which was quite un-Victorian and not quite English.

Though all the component parts of the capital were still recognizably there –

Previous pages: Piccadilly Circus lit by flashing neon advertisements and resounding to the roar of motorized traffic in the 1930s. Known as the Heart of the Empire, it provided a brilliant display of the twentieth-century technology that was changing London's economy as well as Britain's position in the world the West End and its Season; the financial hubbub of the City; grand houses and slums – everything had changed. There seems to have been a loosening of the old social order, a more egalitarian mood which was somehow reflected in the clean, 'modernistic' lines of new office buildings along the Embankment, eschewing the ornate paternalism of the Victorians. Everything was brighter, neater, smarter, electric-lit: at night an illuminated façade proudly displaying the stylish modernity of a new building. Piccadilly Circus, flashing giddily above the subterranean splendour of its Art Deco Underground station, was the ultimate showpiece of this new, nocturnal, neon London.

In the 1920s, when the fabric of the capital began to be renewed, it was generally believed that it was the cataclysmic experience of the Great War which had somehow brought about the transformation of London's Victorian heartland. The entire social order had been shaken up and when it settled again people were different. In their new mood they had set about restructuring the capital and without the war London might have continued to grow and evolve and there would have been no sudden break with the past. Historians continue to argue about the significance of the Great War in the social and economic evolution of Britain: did it change everything, or merely interrupt a constellation of powerful forces which would have transformed it anyway? Though it's an impossible question to answer, it is worth pursuing as the attempt reveals a great deal about London and its history. There is no doubt that between 1914 and 1939 the capital was radically changed. But was it by a threat of invasion from the Kaiser's Germany, or a much more successful invasion of another kind, which began well before 1914 and was led by the nation which was emerging as the leader of a new world economic order, America?

WHEN WAR was declared on 4 August 1914, Britain was for the first time in centuries threatened by direct assault from an enemy. It appears quite bizarre now that the first attack on the Island Fortress was the shelling in December 1914 by German battle cruisers of Hartlepool, Scarborough, and Whitby, leaving 230 people dead and 500 injured. London at that time still seemed to be relatively safe from bombardment, but it was the prize the German army wanted most and they had developed an extraordinary new weapon which they believed would smash the capital into submission and bring about a swift victory. This was the Zeppelin, an enormous gas-filled airship invented by Count von Zeppelin, who had supposedly got the idea while fighting in the American Civil War, in which hot-air balloons had been used for reconnaissance. Before 1914, a peaceful Zeppelin passenger service had been started in Europe.

These airships were extremely cumbersome contraptions which floated along at ten to fifteen thousand feet at a speed of about fifty to sixty miles an hour, their crew suspended in a small carriage below an enormous cigar-shaped gas bag. High winds and bad weather were a great problem for the Zeppelin commanders and they were always being blown off course, snooping around the sky trying to work out where they were. It was some time before the first of them made the long journey from Germany, across Eastern England to London.

For Londoners, the threat of an air attack by these other-worldly craft was uniquely terrifying. The capital had no air defences to speak of – a few Pom-Pom guns left over from the Boer War which were useless, and aircraft which could not at first climb fast or high enough to attack the Zeppelins. There were no air-raid shelters or air-raid warnings to begin with, and the anticipation of bomb attacks was like a futuristic nightmare. When a primitive black-out was organized, Londoners stumbled about peevishly in the gloom, there was a spate of road accidents, and Summer Time was brought in to make better use of the daylight hours.

The first raid on London came at near midnight on 31 May 1915 when a Zeppelin slipped unchallenged, and in fact unnoticed, over East London, and dropped a string of incendiary and explosive bombs and one hand grenade in a line from Stoke Newington, down to Hackney, peppering Stepney, West Ham and Leytonstone on its route back to Germany. Six people were killed and thirty-five injured. From then on, on star-lit nights there was constant vigilance, and though there were few Zeppelin raids on London, the sight of a silver grey airship, lit up by a search-light, became one of the most haunting images of the Great War in London. A fairly primitive warning system was developed, with maroon rockets fired when a Zeppelin was detected on its way to London, and policemen cycling or motoring around with signs saying 'Take Cover'. Boy scouts with bugles sounded the all clear.

THIS HOUSE contains a fairly good sized **CELLAR,** in the event of an **AIR RAID** passers by are welcome to what shelter it affords.

Above: Policemen in cars, and on bicycles, gave warnings with 'Take Cover' notices. When a raid was over, they swapped these for 'All Clear' signs, and boy scouts blew bugles

Left: Damage to Bartholomew Close, off Aldersgate in the City, after a First World War air-raid. Though at first they struck terror into the hearts of Londoners, the Zeppelins and later aeroplane raids were not the deadly weapons that the Kaiser's generals imagined, and had little military impact

Far left: Passers-by being offered a makeshift air-raid shelter in July 1917. By that time there had been a number of Zeppelin raids on London, and a primitive warning system had been developed

People sheltered under kitchen tables, ran into open country, made a dive for the basement if they had one, but more often than not, it seems, could not resist the temptation to stand at the window or in the street to watch the aerial display of a Zeppelin lit up in a searchlight beam, shells exploding around it from a barrage of guns. The airship's engines became a familiar sound to Londoners, 'like a train in the sky'. Michael MacDonagh noted in his diary *In London During the Great War* that the attitude seemed to be: 'You can hear the Zep' afar off, so that when it appears to be coming near you, you can make a bolt for shelter.'

The extraordinary feel of these first air-raids is still recalled by elderly Londoners, and in particular the cosmic event in September 1916 when an airship was shot down by a young pilot over Cuffley in Hertfordshire. Several million Londoners saw the great gas bag turn into a ball of flame, among them G.S. Occomore who was a boy at the time:

> It was about two o'clock in the early hours of Sunday morning, September 3rd. An air raid was on and two other children were under the kitchen table with me, peeping out from underneath, looking up through the window at the searchlights criss-crossing the sky. All of a sudden they got the Zeppelin. It looked like some silver cigar . . . it turned, ducked, weaved, but still the searchlights held it. Suddenly it disappeared behind a cloud and then the searchlights picked it up again. Almost at once the flames shot up from the top of the Zep' and immediately there were shouts and cheers from the streets outside. We all rushed out. But now the Zeppelin was all alight, slowly falling like some burning fiery star. . . .

Con Young can still vividly remember how, as a seven-year-old child, her East End domestic routine – and that of her cat – was suddenly and dramatically disrupted by a direct hit from a Zeppelin bomb.

> We were all in bed. I was asleep in my bedroom with the cat at the foot of my bed in his usual place. My mother, so she told me later, was in her bedroom sitting on the edge of her bed waiting to pick up and set her clock by the 10.00 through-train whistle as it passed the back of our house.
>
> It was the London to Southend train, and it would whistle each night before it went through our station, so it was my mother's habit to check her clock by it. This night she heard the whistle, so she thought, but it was a bomb whistling down through the uncanny silence. The Zeppelins were very quiet, we never heard them, but sometimes we would catch sight of them drifting in the clouds.
>
> I'll never forget that awful night, the bomb dropped behind us, slicing off the backs of the houses in the next road with a deafening crash, and a brilliant green crackling light. Everything moved in that room. My poor cat went past me high in the air and was drawn through the hole where the window had been. My long thick hair saved me from being cut when the broken window frame, bits of door, needles of glass, all sorts of things, flew into my corner on top of me.
>
> By then my mother had managed to get to me and was pulling the debris

off and she picked me up bedclothes and all. She walked through the broken glass with only stockings on her feet, then she dropped me in an armchair just inside where the front room had been, and it was like putting me in the front garden, as it was open to the street. I remember her saying quite calmly, 'Don't worry, it's only the Germans! I will get my shoes', as if it was quite normal to be bombed.

Then came the police, ambulances, firemen, the gas people and people from miles around, and our road was soon packed tight. Nobody could control the crowd, they just walked over the bricks of our front room, all over the house, they were getting wedged in the passages and pushing and shouting and it was still not daylight, but we were powerless – we had to stay just where we were. People were so sorry for us they left money everywhere, and the big glove box on the hallstand was filled with so much money that we had to keep emptying it because it wouldn't close.

Three months went by and we'd searched everywhere and asked everybody about the cat. Then one day, I was picking some beans and he walked up to me in the garden and nobody believed it was him. 'Oh it isn't', they said. 'It's another cat.' But it was him. But he would never come in the house. He came for his food and would eat it in the garden, but he would never enter the house.

The Zeppelin raids on London were, however, in military terms, a failure. In all an estimated 670 people were killed and 1,962 wounded in twelve airship attacks, and nineteen aeroplane raids which came later on in the war. Germany failed to frighten London into submission, or to hit the most prized target in the City, the Bank of England, symbol of Britain's great financial might. But the dimming of lights and the fear of air attack were significant in creating an atmosphere of common peril, and a kind of camaraderie which no previous war had achieved. There was, too, a deeply-felt symbolism in the realization that London was vulnerable, after all those centuries, and Michael MacDonagh recalls the extraordinary occasion when MPs and Peers left the Houses of Parliament to watch a Zeppelin raid from Palace Yard: 'How strikingly it appeals to the historical imagination! The thought in my mind was that England's insularity was at an end, that her Navy could no longer keep her safe from an enemy entry into her Island Fortress.'

So strange was the attack from the air that quite a number of people apparently refused to believe that Zeppelins could really fly all the way from Germany, and their appearance in the sky helped to fuel the witch-hunt on Germans in London, all of whom were suspected of being spies and of sending secret signals to their compatriots. MacDonagh records a conversation his wife had with their charlady, Annie Bolster from Battersea.

'Isn't it an extraordinary thing, Annie,' said my wife, 'that the Zeppelins, great ships like Atlantic liners, should be able to sail through the air from Germany to London and back?'

'Don't you believe it, Ma'am,' Annie replied, 'Don't you believe it. We know in Battersea that these 'ere Zeppelins are hidden away in the back yards of German bakers.' And many a German shopkeeper had his windows smashed and goods looted in the East End.

The Zeppelins may have provided the most haunting image of the Great War, but they did not lead to an evacuation of the capital, or to any dispersal of the war effort, as the threat of the Blitz did in the Second World War. In fact, the 1914-18 War *concentrated* activity in London, for new government departments created to deal with the national emergency grew up around Westminster, in particular the enormous Ministry of Munitions, which by 1918 was employing sixty-five thousand people, and was responsible for around three million workers in engineering, munitions and on the railways. The central part of town teemed with government office workers and soldiers home on leave or returning to the front.

All this activity put a great strain on the transport services, which by then included the electric Tube lines, mostly built between 1900 and 1907. Motor buses, which had just begun to replace horse-drawn vehicles, were commandeered for service on the front. Trams were used as mobile searchlight trollies, and the drivers and conductors were lost as men volunteered, or, after conscription in 1916, were called up. It was mostly after 1916 that women were recruited on a large scale as surrogate men, and appeared on the London streets in unfamiliar guise, as Lloyd George's 'munitionettes', or as bus conductresses and ticket collectors on the Underground or as drivers of delivery vans for Joe Lyons. In the City, the

A group of cheerful women painters who took over 'men's' jobs on the Underground around 1916. The social upheaval that the First World War caused in London had more lasting impact than the air-raids

banks began to train women clerks on an 'experimental basis', as they put it; by the end of the war nearly a third of Lloyds Bank staff were women.

To what extent the experience of the war altered the way in which Londoners thought about, and used, the centre of town is not clear, but there are some intriguing bits of evidence to suggest that it was at this time that the capital really began to develop its contemporary character. In her memoir, *How We Lived Then*, Mrs C.S. Peel dates the rise of Soho as a night-club-cum-popular-restaurant area, which anyone might venture into, from this period when girls, working as government clerks, found it a convenient place to meet off-duty soldiers. The ban on restaurateurs serving officers after 10.00 p.m. with alcoholic drinks – the 'Beauty Sleep' order – gave rise to a whole colony of new night-clubs. And as early as the autumn of 1915, the *Daily Mail* had noted in the centre of town the appearance of a new breed which it called 'Dining Out Girls': 'The war-time business girl is to be seen any night dining out alone or with a friend in the moderate-price restaurants in London. Formerly she would never have had her evening meal in town unless in the company of a man friend. But now, with money and without men, she is more and more beginning to dine out.'

War work took many women out of domestic service, still by far the most important source of employment for them in London in 1914. Just under half the first recruits joining the London General Omnibus Company in 1916 gave domestic service as their previous employment, and though nobody has calculated what the effect was on middle- and upper-class life, it is quite clear that much of the West End and the wealthier parts of London abandoned their formerly flamboyant existence. Their staffs were depleted but, perhaps more important than anything else in this total war, displays of wealth were not acceptable. In the twenties the Season and the household with a substantial number of servants returned, but not on the scale of the Edwardian era.

THE GREAT WAR affected every aspect of London life, and it is quite understandable that the generation who lived through it felt that the changes they saw in the capital in the 1920s were a direct result of those four years of upheaval. In the twenties, morals and manners seemed to become free and easy, personified by the flapper dressed boyishly, smoking a cigarette and dancing to a jazz band at the Savoy. There were those who thought there might be a return to the old ways when the lightheadedness of the post-war days wore off, but by the 1930s it was clear that London was being transformed. And now the over-riding impression was that everything was in one way or another becoming American.

In *London in My Time*, written in 1934, Thomas Burke said:

The bulk of our entertainment is American in quality and largely in personnel. All our latest hotels derive from American models. Our snack-bars and all-night supper-stands are pirated from America. Our electric night-signs are an American idea. Our street songs are American. . . . The American yeast, working constantly these last twenty years, has done so much good that we now regard the zest and pungency of London life, which the States gave us, as our own growth.

An illustration from the original brochure for the Grosvenor House Hotel, opened in Park Lane in 1929. London Society was still very much alive, but entertained much more in hotels – rather than private houses – and hummed to a syncopated, American beat. Note the cocktail glass on the table

It would be quite reasonable to assume that it was the trauma of the First World War and the disruption of the British economy which had allowed in the American invader in the wake of the Zeppelins. But the position of Britain, and London, in the world had been threatened well before 1914, and the foundation of most of the changes which became so evident in the inter-war years had really been laid at the turn of the century. The period from 1890 to 1914 had been one of great international economic, political and imperial rivalry, and though London was still the undisputed leader among great cities of the industrialized world, a change in its position was becoming evident. London's character was transformed between the wars, and in this chapter we will look at the impact of a host of forces on the capital's centre.

It was the West End in particular which began to undergo a series of changes which were to undermine its former character as primarily an aristocratic quarter, built up around the royal court and Parliament. The rise of large department stores, such as William Whiteleys of Westbourne Grove and Harrods of Knightsbridge, had signalled the opening-up and expansion of this part of town from the 1870s onwards. But in the early years of this century the erosion of the West End's exclusivity began to accelerate, and American interlopers played a considerable part in helping it on its way.

The most conspicuous example of the American invasion was the arrival at the western end of Oxford Street of a brand new store, built by Gordon H. Selfridge. It was the creation of an American who had made his fortune in Chicago, having risen from a store boy working in the basement of Marshall Fields to a brilliant manager. Selfridge was in his fifties, and was looking around for a new challenge when he decided to come to London and build a super-store that would shake the dust out of the old capital. Like so many American businessmen in this period, to him London represented a vast untapped market, served as it was by rather old-fashioned tradesmen and antiquated industry. Even the immense new edifice of Harrods, being rebuilt when Selfridge arrived in London, appeared to represent no more than a worthy rival which might soon be overtaken.

A full-page advertisement taken in the *Morning Leader* and the *Evening News* by Gordon H. Selfridge to announce the opening of his new store in Oxford Street in 1909. Selfridge, an American, brought a razzamatazz that was new in London to the running and promotion of his department store, and greatly influenced shopping in the 1920s and 1930s. On the roof was a 'Tea Garden open to the sky', probably the first of its kind in London

It was the received wisdom that the site Selfridge chose for his store, at the run-down western end of Oxford Street, was disastrous. But it was not his intention to build his store in an already established district, such as Knightsbridge or South Kensington: he would create his own fantastic world inside a brand new building, as a kind of late Edwardian Disneyland. The opening of the store in 1909 was preceded by an extravagant promotion, with full-page newspaper advertisements – still relatively novel in Britain – and an invitation to everyone in London to visit without any obligation to buy.

A classic Selfridges' window display in March 1930, when the store celebrated its 21st birthday. Before Selfridge arrived in London, such window displays were relatively rare

The windows along Oxford Street – which were to be added to as Selfridges grew – caused quite a stir as their exotic displays had not been seen in London before, and the fantastic interior included an American soda-water fountain and barber's shop. It was Selfridge's policy that customers should not be harassed by floor walkers, and the free and easy atmosphere of the place was probably the most unfamiliar part about it. At the top of the store was an exotic pergola roof garden, which at various times incorporated a practice range for golfers, a setting for ragtime orchestras and an ice-rink. When the roof was extended in the 1920s, Selfridges could claim to have the largest roof garden in the world.

The magnificent lifts in Selfridges, with their lady attendants dressed in a strange, riding habit outfit. Designed by the Birmingham Guild, these lifts which were splendidly modern in the 1930s are already preserved relics: an example is on show in the Museum of London

Though other stores, such as Harrods and Swan & Edgar, did not seem to take the threat of this interloper too seriously, they did stage fashion shows and concerts of their own as a counter-attraction to this extraordinary opening day. However, it was not long before the American influence was evident throughout the West End, and it really came to prominence after the First World War when many of the established London stores were rebuilt. Large, ground-floor window displays became the rule, as did the open interior shopping areas – a number designed by Americans brought in specially for their expertise.

Today, the Quadrant of Regent Street, which sweeps from Oxford Circus to Piccadilly Circus, does not look to us to be particularly 'modern' or even characteristically 1920s. However, nearly the whole of it was rebuilt after the Great War. By the early 1900s, the stuccoed buildings designed by John Nash in the Regency period were in poor repair, and the Crown, whose property this was and is, began to consider plans for redevelopment. There were great arguments about the Quadrant's design and how the work should be carried out, but only a small part – notably the Piccadilly Hotel – was rebuilt, in grand metropolitan style, before the outbreak of war put an end to the project. It was in the 1920s that most of the rebuilding took place, and the new fashion for large windows, taller buildings constructed on steel frames with stone facings, and much more open-floor plans were brought in.

When it was rebuilt Harrods had incorporated luxury apartments above the showrooms, but these had to be rapidly re-absorbed as the store expanded. Similarly in Regent Street, plans for flats above the shops were abandoned. It was clear evidence that the West End was continuing to lose its residential character, and becoming more and more a national and international shopping centre. The official re-opening of Regent Street in 1927 was marked by a passing visit by King George V and Queen Mary, and the *Daily News* thought that it did 'in a sense typify the spirit of the age – in its vitality and brilliance and audacity. It is more suited to the flashing bus and the rapid streams of polished motor-cars than to the old-fashioned coach-and-four.'

In Kensington, too, the 1920s saw the rise to prominence of Barkers' store. This had been an important shopping area before the 1914-18 War, and by 1920 the Barker Brothers had already bought up their rivals, Pontings and Derry & Toms, though the three stores continued to function as separate businesses.

The electrification of the District Line from 1905, and the redesign of High Street Kensington Station, enabling shoppers to walk straight from the octagonal booking hall into Pontings on one side and Derry & Toms on the other, had given the area a tremendous boost. Rebuilding of Barkers began in 1923, and though it was not completed until 1958, the great ocean-liner style more nearly reflected 'the spirit of the age' than anything in Regent Street.

The splendid 'stripped classical'-style Derry & Toms Store in Kensington, looking its best illuminated at night in 1938. Despite the Depression, department stores in London boomed in the 1920s and 1930s, and Derry & Toms was one of three new buildings put up by Barker Brothers in Kensington High Street between the wars

Here, too, the management looked to American department stores for the interior design, and brought in architects for some of the work. And here, too, the expansion of the store, in particular the demolition of houses next to Kensington Square to make space for staff quarters, and the crowding of the street with shoppers from all over London, began to change the predominantly residential character of the area. In the late 1930s, a roof garden was added to the attractions of Derry & Toms – a bright idea brought originally to London by Gordon Selfridge.

The growth of the new superstores in the West End represented not an entirely new departure, but more a continuation of the evolution of this wealthy part of London from the preserve of the upper classes during the annual round of balls and dinners in the Season into the playground for the whole of London. It was a creeping kind of development which had been going on since the late nineteenth century, marked by the appearance of new kinds of buildings and new forms of shopping and entertainment. The style and tone of much of this was American, because it was in the United States that the mass consumer society had developed first: London, in a way, was catching up.

Hollywood completely dominated the cinema in the inter-war years. Not only were London audiences in the West End entertained by American movies, but much of the exotic picture palace architecture was influenced by American design, though the buildings were actually created by English architects. The black granite Odeon in Leicester Square, which replaced the Alhambra Theatre in 1937, is a good example of such an un-English incursion in the West End. However, the picture palaces in the heart of London's entertainment centre had much less of an impact than those built in the suburbs, where their interior splendour completely overshadowed their surroundings (see Chapter Five).

The significant social influence of the cinema was, first, that it was much cheaper than the theatre, and, second, that it promoted an American culture that was much more accessible to the mass of London's population than previous forms of entertainment. Thus the cinema was to play its part in opening up the West End to many more people. So, too, did the arrival of new chain stores, such as Woolworths – another American import – which got its first foothold in Britain in Liverpool in 1909 and arrived in London with a store in Oxford Street in 1924. And if you look above the jumble of shop fronts in Oxford Street today, you can see in the inter-war design of many of the buildings the relics of thirties' mass consumerism brought in by the likes of Marks & Spencer.

So, from the late nineteenth century onwards, the influence of private wealth was slowly giving way to the more vigorous forces of a new kind of commercial wealth in the West End. And it was in the 1920s and 1930s that the culture and style of the old and new societies were fused in a fascinating and often comical way in this part of London. The landed aristocracy were still rich, but the basis of their wealth was being slowly eroded by taxes, death duties and a fall in the value of the basis of much of their income as agriculture slumped, and coal – out of which many had made fortunes – fell in value. At the same time, the rise of mass consumerism had produced an increasingly powerful new clientele in the West End.

The futuristic, black granite façade of the Odeon, Leicester Square, opened in 1937. Hollywood films dominated entertainment in London between the wars, and cinema architecture was greatly influenced by American design. Film stars came to rival the aristocracy for public attention

Here, too, the Americans – attracted to London by its size, its traditions and its culture – played an important role in the transformation of the capital's high society. Americans had been arriving in London and seeking an entrée in aristocratic society well before the 1920s, and in fact the old established East Coast families had first been accepted back in the 1870s. In the years just before the Great War, American music had captivated London with the ragtime craze, which disturbed a few old colonials like Rudyard Kipling, who remarked that 'one doesn't feel very national when one is hummed at nasally by an alien'. In 1912 *The Times* had called ragtime 'the music of the hustler and the feverishly active speculator'.

But it was in the inter-war years that the American invasion reached its climax with wealthy Americans trying to break into London Society and the ailing aristocracy gradually giving way as well-heeled millionaires pursued their daughters, and transatlantic heiresses found themselves titled husbands. The whole of the Season, the great gathering of the upper crust in the West End, was jazzed up, and social life was played out less and less in grand houses and more and more in the big new hotels, where the music was provided by an American band or by an English favourite, such as Ambrose, who echoed the transatlantic syncopated beat.

The American 'invasion' also had an important effect on the changing architecture of the West End in the inter-war years. The most conspicuous change that took place was the rebuilding of much of Park Lane, where two of the grandest aristocratic mansions, Grosvenor House, home of the Dukes of Westminster, and Dorchester House, were demolished in the 1920s to make way for hotels and flats.

There had been attempts to let Grosvenor House privately in 1919 when the Duke of Westminster decided not to live there any longer. However – and this is absolutely characteristic of the era – an aristocratic tenant was less valuable than the building of the kind of block of hotel and flats that was the latest thing in New York, and which might attract American visitors. In fact,

The new Grosvenor House Hotel, which replaced an aristocratic town house in Park Lane, towering above the family houses of the early nineteenth century. Though the façade of Grosvenor House was the work of Sir Edwin Lutyens, the famous British architect, its conception was American. As well as hotel rooms, there were service apartments on the New York model

A suite in the Grosvenor House Hotel illustrated in the original brochure. The separate entrance hall and *en suite* bathroom were features designed to attract Americans, accustomed to much greater hotel luxury than Londoners. Iced running water was provided in the bathrooms

the speculator who first put up the rebuilding scheme said that the new Grosvenor House was designed specifically to cater for the American market, and though the building may not look very transatlantic to us today, it was the first hotel in London to have a separate entrance lobby to each bedroom, and a separate bathroom with running iced water: a peculiarly American taste. It was the interiors of English buildings in the 1920s and 30s, rather than the façades, that came under American influence.

Two years after Grosvenor House Hotel was completed in 1929, the Dorchester was built on the site of Dorchester House, and it was said that Park Lane was beginning to resemble Fifth Avenue in New York, though perhaps the most obvious connection between the two was the booking office that the Grosvenor House opened in Fifth Avenue to attract American tourists. No skyscrapers were built in London in this period perhaps only because of a regulation laid down in 1894 that no buildings in the capital should rise higher than eighty feet – a ruling which, incidentally, prevented Gordon Selfridge from carrying out his plan to build a St Paul's-type dome on top of his new store.

However, there were still in the 1920s, and even in the 1930s, quite splendid old-style residences surviving, such as Londonderry House at the Hyde Park Corner end of Park Lane. Lord Jessel recalls going to dances there, where one could be attended by five footmen, and the total staff might amount to twenty. But the American hostesses provided rival attractions, and their lavish parties were attended by the aristocracy, who had great fun at the expense of their vibrant but 'uncultured' hosts. There were many stories, perhaps mostly fabricated, but telling nonetheless, about the misunderstandings of American hostesses. Lord Jessel recalls an American hostess who was told that Lord So-and-so had married the hat-check girl from a certain night-club. 'Oh, I don't know the Hatchecks, are they a good family?' the lady enquired.

Lady Charlotte Bonham Carter remembers how Society eagerly embraced the American 'invaders', principally because they injected new life – and money – into an ailing London Season:

> The rich Americans, I think, were interested in our nobility and they were fascinated by Society. We were interested in them because they were so well off. They brought a liveliness to the West End – before they came it had all been rather serious and formal – their approach was to call each other by their Christian names from the word go. They were terribly amusing and they brought the new fashions with them. Cocktail parties, they were all the rage, they were so convenient, you could drop in and didn't have to dress up. Then there was jazz and wonderful reviews with comedy and music.
>
> Life became much more vibrant, and what was particularly noticeable was the change in the way women behaved and the way men behaved towards us. The female became a person in her own right, she was utterly different. Before, a lady of the British leisured classes did not make up, all foreign ladies did and they often looked utterly artificial with a completely painted face, but it was thought to be very bad style if one made up. That changed completely after the war, we all made up, it was a continental thing we adopted. Until then it was the Americans, the French, or Italians who did it. There was so much more freedom for women than before.

It was not, of course, simply the influence of Americans that was changing the aristocratic heart of London. British society was evolving quite rapidly, and the West End of London would have been transformed anyway. The exclusiveness of the aristocratic way of life, set in grand houses around the royal court, had begun to break down in the late nineteenth century, as wealthy capitalists were able to buy their way into fashionable addresses. Even before 1914, it was remarked that Park Lane was becoming rather *nouveau riche*, with businessmen like Barney Banato living there. The landed aristocracy were losing their grip, and struggling a little to maintain their old way of life. On the Duke of Westminster's estate in Mayfair, it was becoming difficult to let large houses in the early 1900s, and hardly any new mansions for single family occupation were built.

Living in flats or apartments was the exception rather than the rule for the wealthy and the poor alike during the nineteenth century. But from the 1880s, luxury flats became fashionable not only in Kensington, but right in the heart of Mayfair. When the area around Mount Street, just at the back of Park Lane, was rebuilt in the 1890s by the Grosvenor Estate, flats were constructed above shop premises. It was already clear that this kind of arrangement would prove much more profitable for a landlord as apartments were easier to let than large houses, and by the 1920s and 1930s the apartment was more or less the only kind of new housing development in the West End. The massive Grosvenor House development on Park Lane included, as well as a hotel, apartments built in the style of New York blocks with a staff of communal servants. This was the system adopted, too, in Grosvenor Square when it was rebuilt from the late 1920s onwards.

Life for the aristocracy became much more streamlined, more attuned to the modern world. Motor cars rapidly replaced horse-drawn carriages in the early 1900s, and the first recorded case of an old stable being converted into a bijou mews house in Mayfair dates from 1908. Cars required fewer servants than carriages, and were in the long run not only faster but cheaper and more efficient. Likewise, the cocktail party was not only very new and fashionable, it was also, according to *Harpers Bazaar*, the cheapest way to entertain. Less and less of the aristocratic social round involved the enormous expense of horses, teams of servants, and massive houses. More and more of it moved to hotels and to night clubs, with the guests whisked from one to another in chauffeur-driven cars. It was still very lavish and very glamorous for those who enjoyed it, but quite different from the old way of life. Lady Marguerite Strickland was one of the great beauties of her day:

> I went to a lot of night clubs every night. The Florida – that was the first night club – was popular with the debs, and that was great fun. The men wore black cloaks and there were telephones on all the tables, so that you could be rung up by a man across the room, it was very romantic. The Florida was semi-dark, but the most popular club was the Four Hundred; everyone loved it because it was completely dark. Then there were The Monsignor, The Embassy, The Nest, The Kit Kat, there were lots and lots of them, and often you didn't know where you were, you'd go from one to another when a party dragged on and it was all dark.
>
> And the idea of the darkness was that you'd be dancing with someone else's husband and your husband was across the room with the man's wife. The dancing was so important, the new band music was so marvellous, I used to know all the tunes and the band leaders who used to play in the clubs were all friends of ours. It was all so exciting.

The old and new ways of life in the West End overlapped. It was generally the dashing younger set who most readily adopted the cocktail, the dance-band, and the Art Deco apartment. A domestic servant might be required to

Above: Lady Marguerite Strickland, a great beauty of the thirties, in her element amongst the Bright Young Things of London Society

Left: The cocktail bar of the Embassy Club in 1933. Although the history of the cocktail as a drink is obscure, its arrival in London in the twenties was part of the Americanization of the West End

move from one world to another, as Stanley Agers discovered when he began work 'below stairs' in Belgrave Square in 1921. On one occasion he might be a footman with powdered hair; on another he was learning to mix a cocktail for the new breed of aristocrat with American friends:

> We had about eighteen staff and my job as steward room boy was really to look after the upper crust of the servants, including the butler, the housekeeper, the lady's maid, the valet, the under-butler, the groom of chambers, and the chef. The people who were struggling to keep going with this way of life were old people like Lord and Lady Coventry, who were really Victorian.
>
> My livery in the daytime would probably be fawn, with a chocolate collar and a striped waistcoat. At nighttime it would be dark blue with a black velvet collar. Any evening, from about eight o'clock onwards there might be two or three dinners going on around the square, and as guests arrived, the red carpet would be out. It lived at the front door and was rolled across the pavement, with a footman stationed outside to stop people walking on it. A big carriage umbrella was also always kept by the front door in case of any rain or pigeons.
>
> By the time the Americans were flooding in, I was second footman in Cadogan Square and my employer was quite, shall we say, one of the Bright Young Things. He had an American publisher and American friends. This was when the cocktails came into the big houses, before that it was all straight drinks. We didn't know anything about mixing cocktails and I was sent round to the Savoy to see one of the barmen. He showed me how to make a proper Martini, and a real winner was a White Lady, which was always made with fresh passion fruit juice, which you could only buy at Fortnum & Masons.
>
> With the Americans it was very difficult for us. They really didn't know how to handle us at all, they were either too friendly or the other way around. They always wanted iced water, and we had no refrigerators, just the old-fashioned ice box. We used to buy our ice by the hundredweight. The only way to keep these people happy was to chip off some of this ice and cool their water that way.

It is extremely difficult to gauge accurately the extent of the shift in the social life of the upper crust in the inter-war years. The Season was still very much alive, and the royal court remained the centre for great occasions, such as the presentation of debutantes. But new occasions were invented which had little or nothing to do with the established social round; the best known being Queen Charlotte's Ball for debs. Much less exclusive than presentation at court, this began in 1922, and though its origin is a little obscure, it was and remained a fund-raising event for Queen Charlotte's Maternity Hospital and had absolutely nothing to do with any social tradition. From the time that the Grosvenor House Hotel was completed in 1929, the Ball was always held there, along with the cardboard cake and the girls all dressed alike, as if they were out of a Hollywood pageant.

At the same time, the position of royalty within British Society was changing, with consequences for London's West End. Though most people imagine that the British have always been masters of royal pageantry, this expertise in fact dates only from the late nineteenth century. Before that, pomp and ceremony often lapsed into the ludicrous and it was the staging of Queen Victoria's Golden Jubilee in 1887 that established the great tradition of British royal ceremonies – at a time when the monarch was losing the last vestiges of real political power and was becoming much more of a national figurehead. Splendid occasions followed: the Diamond Jubilee of 1897, Queen Victoria's funeral in 1901, the coronations of Edward VII and George V in 1902 and 1911, and an area was rebuilt to provide an appropriate setting for the processions. Between 1906 and 1913, from money provided by the Queen Victoria Memorial Fund, Buckingham Palace was refaced and the Mall widened, with Queen Victoria's Memorial at the palace end, and Admiralty Arch by Trafalgar Square. So the stage was set for the fashioning of the monarchy into a kind of theatrical company, which now performs regularly for the world's television cameras and for millions of snap-happy tourists who have become so important to London's economy.

IN THE nineteenth century, it was the square mile of the City itself which had been transformed into London's great commuter centre, as the old shops and housing gave way to Victorian office blocks built to accommodate the armies of clerks and financiers. By the early 1900s, the financial institutions of the City had begun to colonize the area which surrounded the old square mile. But the City had by this time reached its historical zenith, and though it made a remarkable recovery from the destruction of its overseas investments in the Great War, and much of it was rebuilt in the inter-war years, it was not a major force in the expansion of central London employment. This came from quite a new direction, and, as with so much else in the twentieth century, was triggered off and driven from overseas.

   In international economics, there were two great rivals to Britain in the years before 1914: Germany, which had developed systematically state support and a highly trained, scientifically-based industrial structure powerful in the manufacture of chemicals and new technology; and America, the birthplace of the new consumer society, where mass production techniques, backed by aggressive advertising methods, supplied a mass market of relatively well-paid workers. By the early 1900s these two rival economies began to look to Britain, and London in particular, as a great potential market for their goods and their investment. Britain's industry was, in contrast, for the most part relatively antiquated, fragmented and ill-organized.

   The first great shock to British pride came in 1901 when the giant American Tobacco Company attempted to buy up the British industry. A flamboyant 'Yankee' – a popular term of abuse at the time – called James Buchanan ('Buck') Duke arrived in Liverpool, went straight to the firm of Ogdens and bought it. A fierce battle ensued in which the British industry banded together to beat off the American invader, and for weeks the newspapers were full of pages of aggressive advertising from both sides attempting to win public support. A piece of British doggerel ran:

>   Don't be gulled by Yankee bluff
>   Support John Bull with every puff!

A formidable line-up of American business magnates, with James Buchanan – or 'Buck' – Duke, holding straw hat and cigar, leading the way. Duke's giant company, American Tobacco, tried to buy the British tobacco industry in the early years of the century

In the end, the British manufacturers formed themselves into a giant consortium, the Imperial Tobacco Company, carved out the home market and came to an agreement with the Americans on which of them had control of what part of the world. A new company, British American Tobacco, was formed and built itself a brand new headquarters at Westminster House on Millbank in 1915.

In the inter-war years the pattern of foreign challenge from America, or sometimes Germany, represented the catalyst in pushing British industry into the formation of giant companies to compete on the world market. The whole process was greatly helped by the experience of the Great War, when the need to manufacture armaments killed off the old liberal philosophy of 'free competition' and a belief in the benefits of having a small number of rival firms. The enormous Ministry of Munitions brought together for the first time civil servants and businessmen, and former commercial competitors had to work alongside each other. This experience, which brought home the benefits of large-scale organization as well as the challenge from abroad, made 'rationalization' all the rage in the 1920s and 30s. And the result was the emergence in London of enormous office blocks, employing a new type of commuter working in management and corporate clerical departments.

A survey of the present-day north side of the Thames Embankment shows the enormous structure of Imperial Chemical House almost rivalling its neighbour, the House of Commons, in stature, built as the headquarters of ICI which was formed in response to the challenge of the German chemical industry. Going east, Shell-Mex House and Unilever House are further great symbols of inter-war rationalization, built in the latest architectural style with touches of Art Deco as headquarters for the new corporations.

Such totems to the new corporate age arose all over central London, and might be said to include Broadcasting House in Portland Place, home of the British Broadcasting Corporation, created essentially by government intervention to prevent the free-for-all of American commercial radio, which Lord Reith and others had found so distasteful. In 1940, with its overseas department expanding rapidly, the BBC took over part of Bush House,

Above: One of the classic big corporation office blocks of the inter-war years. Shell-Mex House, under construction on the north bank of the Thames on the site of the old Cecil Hotel. The amalgamation of British business and industry was a feature of the twenties and thirties and gave rise to many such totems of the new corporate society

Left: The art of the new inter-war corporatism: sculpting details for Imperial Chemical House, headquarters of ICI, which was opened in 1928

another wonderful monument of the era. It was the brainchild in 1919 of an American, Irving T. Bush, who designed it as a trade centre, and was finished in 1935. The enterprise proved a failure, but the building was quickly colonized by institutions which were to become essential to the new economy of central London.

The combined effects of the growth of the corporate economy and the apparatus of the new consumer economy were greatly to swell the amount of office work available in central London. The capital's economy benefited enormously from the foreign invasion, while the areas of Britain still dependent on the now antiquated economy of coal and heavy engineering went into decline. Whereas before the First World War, only about a fifth of the largest companies in Britain had headquarters in London, about half of them did by 1935.

So London's middle-class population, swelled in the previous century by the growth of the City and of all the professions that served the old square mile, the government and the West End, was sustained in the inter-war years by the growth of the corporate economy. The much greater state intervention in public affairs also increased the number of civil servants, while the growing importance of local government – symbolized by the rise of County Hall on the South Bank opposite the Houses of Parliament – further added to the demand for white collar workers.

One of the clearest indications of the way in which the West End of London was opening up to new kinds of office workers and to a wider range of shoppers was the growth of modestly-priced restaurants, the most famous being the Joe Lyons chain of tea shops and Corner Houses. These became a kind of lower-middle-class institution, a genteel oasis for the typist or clerk at lunchtime, and for the cinema-goer at night.

Like so much else in the story of inter-war London, the origins of mass catering go right back to the mid-Victorian period. In the 1870s, the capital was badly served with cafés, particularly for the day visitor not wealthy enough to belong to a gentlemen's club and not wishing to partake in the unsavoury fare offered in pubs and chop houses. The situation was especially difficult for women who had to brave a rough-house atmosphere if they wanted any refreshment.

The first efforts to improve catering in London came from the Temperance Movement, which wanted to provide an alternative to the public house. They opened coffee houses, of which there were a hundred in London by 1879, but most of them seem to have been badly run and lasted only a short time. More successful were the purely commercial caterers who applied the techniques of mass production in food to the problem of eating out. The Aerated Bread Company and the Express Dairy opened hundreds of milk and bun shops in the late nineteenth century. At the same time, more expensive restaurants were being established to offer the novelty of a place where a man might take his wife out to supper.

It was in this social context that Joe Lyons first emerged. The firm was founded by Salmon and Gluckstein, who were tobacconists who wanted to branch out into a new line of business, and its first venture was to provide the catering at the Newcastle Exhibition of 1887. It took the name Joe Lyons when it was formed as a public company in 1894. The name comes from a relatively minor figure in the venture, Joseph Lyons, who through his family connection with the Glucksteins was invited to join the company.

The first tea shop in London was established at 213 Piccadilly in 1894, and the first of the plusher, though still inexpensive, Corner Houses was opened in 1909 at the corner of Coventry Street and Rupert Street. Before 1914, the tea shop business expanded rapidly and Lyons' competitors in the field of mass catering were left behind. By the 1920s, Lyons had 250 tea-shops nationally, and its three London Corner Houses could each seat up to three thousand people. It was in this era that Lyons really became established as a national institution, and its waitresses – who were given the nickname 'Nippies' in 1925 – were regarded as the perfect 'public' servants. In the Corner Houses, Londoners on quite modest incomes could enjoy an evening out with live music, cheap but wholesome food, and a degree of luxury in decor which seemed spectacular at the time.

But Lyons did not confine themselves to tea shops and Corner Houses: as early as 1896 they had opened the Trocadero, a high-class restaurant in Piccadilly Circus; they built the Strand Palace Hotel, on the Strand, in 1909; the Regent Palace, at the back of Regent Street, in 1915; and the Cumberland Hotel, at the junction of Oxford Street and Park Lane, in 1933. And, more profitably, they became the leaders in the mass production and packaging of food – particularly of tea, ice-cream, and cakes and buns. Their production centre was at Cadby Hall near Olympia, and in 1931 they were boasting that 500,000 rolls were daily despatched from the bakery there while 160 million meals were served in their restaurants, Corner Houses and tea shops during that year.

By the 1930s, Joe Lyons' catering was already on the wane, as the shorter

A 'Nippy' standing outside production headquarters at Cadby Hall, Kensington, watching cakes and buns being loaded into one of Lyons' fleet of delivery vans

working day took away the breakfasts and teas that they had once served to office workers, and more firms provided meals in canteens. It was the food manufacturing side of the business that thrived. However, Lyons was synonymous by then with a new way of life in London's neon-lit West End, and as the Nippy whisked around the Corner House, she might be chatted up by a group of ordinary lads on a night out, or by a more elevated customer, as Dora Dyers remembers:

When you were a Nippy, you always got somebody that took a little bit of a fancy to you, and once I used to have a very elite gentleman sat at my table. One day, when he went out, he left his card, and much to my amazement he was the Consul General for Brazil. Anyway, the next time he came in he asked if I would go to dinner with him. He was an older man, but I did go and he took me to the Savoy and I had a wonderful time, I felt like a queen.

And I met the man who was to become my husband when I was working at Lyons as well. There was a group of men came in, they'd been playing cricket, and I could tell from their conversation they took it in turns to ask girls they met out. Well it wasn't my husband's turn, but he said 'I don't care even if I fall out with you, I'm going to take this one home', and that was the start of our romance.

Mass consumerism was to have its effect on every level of London Society. The upper classes retained their glamour, and a Society wedding might still draw crowds of sightseers anxious to get a glimpse of the latest fashions, but the allure of the aristocracy was rapidly being eclipsed by that of Hollywood film stars, who were setting the pace and increasingly influencing fashion. In the thirties a beautiful debutante, dashing about in sports cars, spending every night at the Kit Kat Club or The Embassy, was almost like a film star, fêted in the popular newspapers. As a result she would be sought after by advertisers – particularly those from America – to promote a cosmetic, a cigarette or a drink for the mass market. The advertising agency, J. Walter Thompson – which set up office in the 1920s in Bush House – recruited flocks of young aristocratic Ladies to promote Ponds Cream. Among them was Lady Strickland:

When I was eighteen I had a letter from Ponds offering fifty pounds to do an endorsement. That was a fortune to me because, due to a very bitter divorce, I wasn't living with my father and had no money. So I did it and my picture went in the paper more or less straightaway. My father must have seen it, because I had a telegram from him saying it was disgusting and to send the money back, which of course I refused to do. Then later on I did more advertisements, one of them was for Gordon's Gin, although I told them at the time that I never drank alcohol because I disapproved of it. I only drank milk at nightclubs.

No image captures the face of London's heartland in the thirties better than Lady Strickland's memory of her own photograph ablaze at night in Piccadilly Circus, advertising Horlicks:

There was a picture of me up in Piccadilly Circus, about thirty feet high, with a spotlight on it. And it had written across it. 'Do You Suffer From Night Starvation?' One evening Jimmy Horlick and my father were going past in a taxi and Jimmy Horlick, not knowing who the picture was of, because my name wasn't on it, asked, 'Have you seen my advertisement up there?' My father replied, 'Yes, that's my daughter'.

It was up very high and we used to drink its health in milk at four in the morning, after we'd been nightclubbing. Then we'd go off into the country.

LADY MARGUERITE STRICKLAND

Says "A good cocktail *must* be made with **Gordon's Gin**"

THE HEART OF A GOOD COCKTAIL

NO COLOURING MATTER

Lady Marguerite Strickland was one of many aristocratic young women recruited by advertising agencies to promote such products as drinks, cigarettes and cosmetics. The Old Guard of London Society thought such use of titles shocking, but it was exciting and lucrative for a young beauty. Lady Strickland was, and is, teetotal and has never smoked

CHAPTER TWO

EMPIRE AND ELECTRICITY

I F A Londoner were asked today to pick a single monument which had its origins in a celebration of imperialism, they would be unlikely to choose Wembley Stadium, set as it is in a sea of surburban, North London semi-detached houses. But this concrete stadium, which because of its sporting associations is probably the best known building of the inter-war period in London, is a relic of the most lavish and exotic display of the cultural and economic riches of the British Empire ever staged in the capital. The stadium is, in fact, almost the only survivor in Wembley of that spectacular exhibition, for the site soon became an entertainment-cum-industrial district, characteristic of a mass of new development which grew up around London between the world wars. Now it's known as the home of the Cup Final and of horse shows, its imperial history forgotten.

The 1924 British Empire Exhibition, for which the stadium was built, put Wembley well and truly on the map of London. But the exhibition is of more than parochial interest: the story of how it came to be there, what it was meant to achieve, and what eventually happened provides a colourful illustration of the way in which London remained a thriving metropolis between the wars, while the rest of Britain floundered economically as the foundations of its nineteenth-century industrial wealth began to crumble. London was still, in the inter-war years, the capital city of an enormous empire which continued to grow in size until 1937, its territory extended by the conquests of the First World War and piecemeal additions after it. But what proved ultimately much more important for London's continuing prosperity was the fact that it became the most powerful magnet in Britain for new industries, many of them first developed in America. The imperial capital itself was, in a sense, the happy victim of a kind of economic colonization which brought it a new kind of wealth.

The idea for an Empire Exhibition of some kind seems to have been suggested first in the early 1900s, at the time when American and German businessmen and industrialists were making forays into the British market. Even at that early date there was a sense that the riches of the empire, which had historically reflected British economic superiority, might now be harnessed to preserve the nation's position in the face of fierce foreign competition, though there does not seem to have been any great awareness in Britain about what was really going on. American and German manufacturers had been making inroads into the markets of the empire since the late nineteenth century; Britain was already living on borrowed time. The idea for an Empire Exhibition was put forward again in 1914, but the outbreak of war soon put an end to the plans.

When in 1920 an Empire Exhibition was proposed yet again, the world had changed. At a meeting in the Mansion House on 7 June the assembled dignitaries gathered to endorse the enterprise – first put forward by two

Previous pages: Henly's Garage and showrooms on the Great West Road in the 1930s, lit up at night and evoking the new prosperity of London between the wars. Electricity, motor cars and new roads altered the nature of industry and allowed expanding firms to cluster around the capital

private companies which became the British Empire Exhibition Incorporated – saw it at once as a victory celebration and a chance to promote empire trade. Sir Robert Thorne, President of the Board of Trade, captured the mood well when he said that the manifestation of the power of the empire in the war had perhaps been the most remarkable fact in all human history: but he would not talk about that. 'I wish to speak on the business side of the project.' The post-war economic boom would soon be over, he warned, and the time might come when 'trade will sag, and when we may come very near the point of depression'. If that happened, the empire – and Britain – could do with all the trade it could generate.

There was an understandable and, as it turned out, quite justified concern behind the exhibition. It was not, as Viscount Milner, Secretary of State for the Colonies, emphasized, mere 'vainglorious display'. It was hoped that, by bringing together the immense natural resources of its empire, Britain might survive in a much tougher world.

In many ways, the design and mood of the British Empire Exhibition reflected perfectly Britain's ambiguous position between the wars, when new technology was undermining its dominant world position, yet it remained a great imperial nation. The exhibition's siting in Wembley, on the fringes of the built-up area of north-west London, located it in what was to become one of the great boom districts during the worst years of the Depression.

Wembley Stadium was the first exhibition building to go up, and became a showpiece of inter-war modernity. About two thousand men were employed

Not the aftermath of a football riot at Wembley, but a unique picture of the method used by the builders of the concrete stadium to test its structure. Sir Robert McAlpine marched some of the workmen and a platoon of soldiers around the terraces to make sure it was sound before it was opened for the Cup Final in 1923

to put up the reinforced concrete structure, and some of them were marched around the newly-completed terraces – along with a platoon of soldiers – to test its strength. The stadium was able to cope with the vast crowds who attended the Cup Final held there in 1923 when the admission system went wrong and thousands of football fans spilled onto the pitch, holding up the start of the game in which Bolton Wanderers beat West Ham 2-0.

It was in the following year, 1924, that the exhibition proper opened; the whole 216-acre site amounting to a kind of Imperial Disneyland. To illustrate the theme of the empire's resources there were recreations of African villages, a replica of the Taj Mahal, and a scale model of a West Indian waterfall. Central to the Canadian contribution were life-sized, refrigerated sculptures of the Prince of Wales in butter. There were also vast Palaces of Engineering and of Industry. As with all exhibitions, it attracted a great deal which represented the height of modernity, such as the 'all-electric house' – still a rarity. But the section which prophetically seems to have caught the imagination of the vast number of visitors – seventeen million in the first year – was the amusement park. Here, America – the bit of the empire Britain had lost long ago – introduced the first dodgem cars, and a roller coaster. And when the exhibition was held again in 1925, among the displays was Henry Ford's assembly line for mass producing cars. Wembley, in the end, might easily have been a celebration not of empire, but of the new consumerism which was invading Britain.

The Amusement Park, with roller coaster, at the British Empire Exhibition staged at Wembley in 1924. Though the exhibition was supposed to boost Empire trade, it probably did more to introduce Londoners to an exciting future of electrically-powered industry. When the exhibition was over, the ruins of the site became an industrial estate

For the Empire Exhibition did little or nothing for Britain's economy: its lasting effect was to help lay the foundations for a part of London's extraordinary manufacturing success between the wars. After its second year, the exhibition closed down, and a large number of its buildings were handed back to the nations which owned them, or were sold for scrap. They were designed as temporary accommodation, and quite a number were dismantled for use elsewhere. The Palestine Pavilion became a Glasgow laundry, East Africa's a furniture factory, Sierra Leone's a restaurant in Ireland and New Zealand's a dance hall. This asset stripping was carried out by a man who had arrived at the exhibition to run a small cigarette kiosk, and managed to get the demolition contract when it was over. Arthur Elvin eventually scraped the money together to buy Wembley Stadium, which remained like a ship stranded in a sea of dereliction, and made a profit not from football but from greyhound racing.

There were one or two grand plans for the use of the site, such as the proposed British Hollywood, but none of them came about. Instead, the area was colonized, bit by bit, as manufacturers searching for suitable factory sites close to London moved in. The remaining shed-like exhibition buildings, the open aspect of the area, the new roads that had been created to handle the traffic into Wembley, the railway, and the relatively low rents combined to make the exhibition site almost perfect for industrial growth in the 1930s. For Wembley, no more than a small piece of Metroland – middle-class housing development promoted in north-west London by the electrified Metropolitan Line Railway Company – was perfectly situated on the fringes of a metropolis enjoying an extraordinary prosperity in an historical period remembered chiefly for unemployment and industrial decline.

London was a boom town within declining Britain. While the old, coal-based heavy industries of Wales and the North East of England, which had been the basis of nineteenth-century industrial wealth, were seriously threatened by foreign competition, the new consumer industries, mostly electrically-powered and relatively small-scale, grew enormously. Even during the worst years of the slump, from 1929 to 1931, a host of relatively cheap, mass-produced goods made their appearance – many of them have a familiar ring today. Gillette razor blades, Smiths crisps, Marconi radios, Hoover vacuum cleaners, 'silk' stockings made of rayon (manufactured from wood pulp), canned foods, gramophone records were all being churned out for the mass market, promoted by new forms of advertising in popular daily newspapers, in the cinema and on radio.

London was the single greatest consumer market in Britain, and one of the most valuable in the world, because of its immense size, with a population approaching eight million in the mid-1930s. Throughout the previous century London had been, in fact, the largest manufacturing region in the country, and its industries concentrated on satisfying the needs of the metropolis. But in the consumer boom of the inter-war years it moved even further ahead of the field. Between 1923 and 1939, something like *two-thirds* of the new jobs in Great Britain were created in Greater London. And nine hundred new firms, employing twenty-five or more people, were set up in the London area between 1932 and 1938, about half the national total during that period.

London tightened its historic grip on the national wealth, and by the end of the inter-war period government committees were inquiring into the causes of this great regional imbalance.

Droves of jobless descended on the capital in search of work: immigration from the rest of Britain added 600,000 to London's population between the wars. Many were single men who travelled long distances hoping to get a job on spec'. Having little or no money, the newcomers developed their own community networks in the capital, enabling friends and relatives to get jobs, and if necessary helping them to dodge the train fare to London which many could not afford, as Billy Rounce from Jarrow remembers:

When I finished my time after six and a half years as an apprentice shipwright, I had five days' work and then six and a half years on the dole. From the age of twenty-two to twenty-eight, I was out of work. And there were thousands of us on the dole and we wanted a job more than anybody can understand. The best prospects were in London at that time but it was getting there was the problem; the lads couldn't afford to go to London.

So, the only way there was to dodge the fare and the dodge was done by the platform ticket trick. You got the platform ticket at this end, the Newcastle end, and you got on the station, you got on the train and you had a mate meet you with a London platform ticket at King's Cross. Or on a more official basis, one of the lads who did the trip regularly would supply you with a King's Cross platform ticket for a couple of bob. I went down to London doing this and I worked with some of our lads who got me a job on a block of flats in Mornington Crescent.

All the people from Jarrow lived in different parts of London, but if you

The best-remembered march of the unemployed in the inter-war years, the Jarrow Crusade of 1936, on its way into London. Many marchers from declining Tyneside – such as John McNulty (holding banner on the left) – had already been to London looking for work. For the capital got the lion's share of new employment in the thirties and drew in hundreds of thousands of people from depressed areas of Britain

fell sick or if you felt you could do with a handout, you always knew where to go – the path leading to Speaker's Corner on Hyde Park, and the seventh lamp on the left if you were going away from Speaker's Corner.

One of the most poignant stories of the period is of the Jarrow marches from Tyneside to London in 1936, to draw government attention to their desperate condition. The marchers met their sweethearts and relatives in Trafalgar Square, the women having moved down to work as domestics, factory hands or clerks. Indeed many of the marchers themselves were not seeing London for the first time – they had made the journey by train in previous years, seeking out whatever work was going in the boom town of the Depression years, as John McNulty recalls:

It wasn't the first time we'd been to London – the majority of the lads had been before, you'd come down on spec' to look for work. I'd worked on the Great West Road for six weeks, putting the drains in. There was a lot of Geordies, and Irish and Welsh working as navvies, hardly any Londoners though. But when we got into London, I remember, it was pouring with rain, and my mother and my two sisters were at Marble Arch waiting for us to come past – they'd been down in London for some time, working. I made a dash across to them and hugged them. Then we marched on to Hyde Park, there were crowds of people there, and a well wisher gave me on old wireless. Of course, I brought that back on the train with us. We never had a wireless before, we were one of the only ones in our street with one, everyone was coming in to listen to it after that.

In contrast with the rest of the country, which, with the exception of the Midlands, was in decline, the prosperity of London and the South East was visibly quite striking in the 1930s. It made a sharp impression on the novelist and broadcaster, J.B. Priestley, whose book *English Journey* is a vivid account of a tour he made in the mid-1930s.

Priestley contrasted nineteenth-century England, which had been built on coal, iron, steel, cotton, wool and railways, and now provided a landscape of 'Sham Gothic churches, Town Halls, mills and foundries . . . cindery waste ground, mill chimneys . . . and sooty dismal little towns' with modern England. Whereas the old 'is not being added to and has no new life poured into it', the new was growing fast, and as he crawled back into London in a chauffeur-driven car, fog-bound on the Great North Road, he could conjure up in his mind's eye this odd, futuristic world obscured by the mist:

If the fog had lifted, I knew that I should have seen this England all round me at the northern entrance to London, where the smooth wide road passes between miles of semi-detached bungalows, all with their little garages, their wireless sets, their periodicals about film stars, their swimming costumes and tennis rackets and dancing shows. . . . You need money in this England, but you do not need much money. It is a large-scale, mass-production job, with cut prices. You could almost accept Woolworth's as its symbol.

Like many other observers, Priestley found it hard to define this post-First World War England, and resorted to a kind of catalogue of consumerism in order to capture its spirit: 'Cocktail bars, motor-coaches, wireless, hiking, factory girls looking like actresses, grey-hound racing and dirt tracks, swimming pools, and everything given away for cigarette coupons.' He thought it all 'belonged more to the age itself than to this particular island' and imagined its birthplace must be America.

This new world, which was so characteristic of the London created between the wars, was in fact the product of a host of technological changes which had begun to take shape in the late nineteenth century, and came to fruition in the 1930s. They amounted to a second industrial revolution, pioneered in America and by chance particularly favourable to London.

The development of electricity was, indirectly, one of the most important of these technological changes. Though the nature of electricity was understood several centuries ago, its practical application goes back to the early nineteenth century when the electric telegraph first came into use. It was as early as 1848 that its use for lighting was first demonstrated in London when battery-powered arc lamps lit up a part of Trafalgar Square. In the later part of the century, electricity was mainly employed for lighting, generated by small and usually inefficient stations on site. The Savoy Hotel was electrically lit in the 1890s, as were some expensive blocks of flats such as Kensington

An electricity supply company showroom in the 1930s. The industry manufactured for the new consumer markets, thus producing a boom between the wars

Court. The first large-scale generating stations were developed by local authorities for street lighting and by the tramway and railway companies to replace horse or steam power. Before the First World War, Lots Road power station on the Chelsea Embankment was built to run the new electric tubes, and Greenwich power station for the London County Council's newly electrified tramways.

A good deal of electrical inventiveness went on in Britain during the pioneer days, the work of brilliant individuals such as Michael Faraday, Sebastian de Ferranti and Charles Merz. But in the crucial decades just before the Great War, electricity's practical application was hampered. For one thing, the political ideal of *laissez-faire* – or free competition – led the early law-makers to ensure that electricity supply was fragmented, with each licensee allotted only a small area of operations. As the supply of electricity is a classic industry in which large-scale production brings considerable advantages, this proved a setback. Britain also had ample supplies of coal, and there was little incentive to experiment with new forms of power in industry, while the new electricity undertakings had to wage a fierce battle with the gas industry, which competed for the claim to be the truly 'modern' fuel, both in the home and in the factory.

As a result, the development of electrical equipment and its use was not as rapid or dynamic in Britain as it was in the United States or Germany, where neither the law nor traditional reliance on coal presented the same obstacles. British firms wanting to use electric machinery often had to import the equipment from abroad, but even then they were in trouble if they did not have their own power stations, for there was a mass of suppliers. In Greater London in 1917 there were seventy companies and local authorities supplying electricity to the public, with seventy generating stations, fifty different types of systems and twenty different voltages.

It is understandable, then, that a factory inspector should lament in 1901 that: 'in the age of steam this country led the way, whereas in the age of electricity we seem to follow America and other countries'. The foothold the Americans gained early on in the electric revolution coloured much of its future development in London and elsewhere, and was yet another strand in the 'Americanization' of life between the wars.

The experience of the Great War, however, helped to shake Britain out of its archaic approach to the use of electricity. In the manufacture of munitions, the great value of electrically-driven machinery was recognized, and during the four years of the war the output of the industry was doubled. Electricity was essential for new munitions works set up away from coal supplies, often on the north-east and north-west fringes of London. In fact, about ninety per cent of the First World War munitions factories were electrically run, proving the value of this new form of power where new plants had to be set up rapidly.

The war experience was a catalyst, but there is no doubt that electricity would anyway have been rapidly adopted by industry as the major source of power because of its tremendous flexibility in driving machinery. It was the legal and political tangle in which the emergent electrical industry had got itself embroiled that held things up, and ensured that it was not until after the war that the revolution in industrial power took place. The generation and supply of electricity were divided, so that there were power companies which produced the current and a mass of small firms and municipal authorities which sold it.

Left to its own devices, the industry would no doubt have rapidly centralized as strong companies drove out the weak, but this was still not regarded as politically acceptable in the 1920s. A committee investigated the ludicrous state of an industry which had dozens of different frequencies, hundreds of small power stations not used to capacity, and a host of localized 'systems' for pooling power and selling it. The Weir Report came up with the obvious answer: to get rid of the inefficient stations, standardize the system nationally, and connect new, and larger power stations through a 'national gridiron', which quickly became known as the National Grid.

The Electricity Supply Act of 1926 did not, in fact, get rid of the fragmented system but it did set up the Central Electricity Board (CEB) which had the task of superimposing on the existing muddle some kind of order. It set about establishing the National Grid and standardizing the whole system, so that the first stage of the grid was in operation by 1933.

It was not the CEB's job to generate electricity: it bought it from power supply companies, and there was no nationalization of the industry until 1948. In the inter-war years, the grid was not effective in creating a truly national system, with power stations in rural or coastal areas supplying the big cities. Inevitably, therefore, as the demand for electricity both industrially and domestically grew enormously in the twenties and thirties, London required massive new power stations. The siting of these was critical as water was needed for cooling the generators, and along the Thames – once the main highway for coal barges bringing London's fuel – new cathedrals of the electric age were built.

Battersea Power Station, now as much a landmark as St Pancras Station and a great symbol of what might be called the 'early modern' industrial age, was planned by the London Power Company in 1927. It was designed by the celebrated architect, Sir Giles Gilbert Scott, and opened in 1931, its giant chimneys fitted with sulphur extractors to reduce pollution in the surrounding area. Battersea Power Station is now becoming a relic of industrial archaeology, but was regarded as the most advanced generator in Europe in the 1930s, and represents that period in the rationalization of industry when the benefits of large-scale production were recognized. Yet nationalization was still not politically acceptable.

The fact that industry was rapidly becoming electrically powered, and that London could supply its own current, greatly encouraged the colonization of the outskirts of the capital by new firms. London's great strength as a manufacturing region had always been that it provided the richest market in Britain, and one of the wealthiest in the world for consumer products. A large part of its industry was small-scale, tucked away in backstreets and alleys. In the 1920s, and to a greater extent in the 1930s, much of this cramped industry was searching for new sites not far from London, but with room to expand. At the same time, new mass production techniques and the growth of electrical products created a great many new firms in search of convenient and economic sites close to London. These two developments laid the

foundations for the capital's spectacular inter-war industrial expansion, which spread right round London but was particularly strong in the north-west around Wembley and the area known as Park Royal.

Most of this region was ideal for firms moving out of the centre, or for those setting up for the first time, because it was largely open country with some of the services required by industry already available. Park Royal provides the classic example. It takes its name from a Royal Agricultural Society showground established on the site before 1914: outside the enormous Guinness factory built there in the late 1930s stand two oak trees planted in 1903 by Edward VII and by the Prince of Wales. As a showground it was apparently a failure, and during the First World War parts of it were used as munitions factories and as a horse compound for the Royal Army Service Corps.

Park Royal was served by the Great Western Railway, which owned a good deal of the land, and the Grand Union Canal. After the Great War, former munitions factories which had been built around the fringes of London were quickly colonized by firms moving out of the centre. This happened at Park Royal, and the story of one firm – Allnatt's – provides an example of the way in which the process worked. Major Allnatt was a caterer from Reading, who took over some disused munitions sheds at the time of the Empire Exhibition to provide food and accommodation for children visiting Wembley in 1924 and 1925. When the Exhibition finished, he realized there was a demand for factory space, and decided to build a small unit for lease. The first road he laid out was named after his foreman, Mr Gorst, and retains that name today. As demand picked up he built more and more small factory units and was completing one every two weeks by the 1930s. By Gorst Road is Standard Road, named after Standard Motor Cars, who were the first firm to arrive there, and Minerva Road, similarly christened because Minerva Cars were the first leaseholders. Allnatt went on to build factories on the Great West Road, and made a fortune out of the inter-war industrial boom.

The Park Royal district of West London, just south of Wembley Stadium, was by the late 1930s one of the single greatest concentrations of industry in Britain. Just after the First World War, most of this was open land: the massive Guinness brewery in the foreground was built on a former Royal Agricultural Society showground

Park Royal lies just to the south of Wembley Stadium, the abandoned site of which was colonized by firms mostly supplying the London market. Wembley was especially favoured because new roads had been laid to cope with the visitors to the Empire Exhibition, and very soon the whole of the area was to benefit from an extraordinary programme of road building linking the new industrial areas with the centre at the very moment of great expansion for motorized transport. Although canals and railways remained important for bringing in bulk raw materials, new roads were revolutionizing goods transport in Britain. In and around London, roads were generally in bad shape before the Great War. The long-distance highways linking the capital with other main cities had gradually fallen into disrepair during the second half of the nineteenth century as the railways creamed off the goods and passenger traffic of the stage coaches. All the turnpike trusts, which maintained the roads by tolls, had gone bankrupt through lack of traffic. The road system, if it could be called that, was administered by a hopeless confusion of authorities, with no incentive to spend money to aid through traffic. At the same time, in central London traffic had increased enormously, and congestion was a serious enough problem to be made the subject of a Royal Commission of Inquiry in 1905. However, the Commission's proposals for reorganizing the administration of roads and the building of new central thoroughfares were largely ignored. And it reported, as Fate would have it, just at the time when a new form of transport, the motor vehicle, was beginning to make its impact on the capital and the country.

The Royal Commission did, however, lead to the formation of the London Traffic Branch of the Board of Trade, which had few powers but was at least able to formulate some kind of policy for future road building. In 1907, this small outfit commissioned a survey of the traffic problem from Colonel Hellard, and the basis of future road policy started to take shape. It was evident then that motor traffic was beginning to overtake horse-drawn traffic in central London. A survey in Westminster, comparing the flow of vehicles in 1903 and 1908 at selected points, revealed that the number of private horse carriages and cabs going by had fallen from 43,790 to 29,967, while the flow of private motor cars had risen from 1,064 to 6,961 and of motor taxis had risen from zero to 19,718. Because motor vehicles were nippier and smaller than horse-drawn vehicles, it was duly noted that the 'change from horse to motor cabs is distinctly beneficial to traffic'.

At the same time, there was a noticeable increase in vehicles in outer London which was 'almost entirely attributable to the growth of mechanical traffic'. In other words, the Traffic Branch appears to have come to the conclusion that the real problem to be solved was in outer London, where the approach routes to the capital through the narrow main streets of outlying suburbs, such as Brentford, were very congested. Schemes for cutting new avenues through central London were pushed into the background, perhaps because it was thought that the motor vehicle was beginning to solve the problem by its superiority over horse-drawn vehicles.

In 1909, the Development and Road Improvement Act provided an important step towards the solution of the tricky problem of how new roads were to be financed, and who was to plan them. In his budget speech, the

A traffic jam in Brentford High Street in the early 1900s. This was a classic bottle-neck on the fringe of Victorian London, causing traffic problems which the new road-building programme was intended to solve. Brentford By-pass was to become the Great West Road

Chancellor of the Exchequer, Lloyd George, brought in motor vehicle and petrol taxation, which was to be used to finance new road building – the Road Fund – and with the act a Road Board was created to administer the fund. There followed a series of Greater London Arterial Roads Conferences and in a patchy and very muddled way a kind of plan emerged to build a network of new, wide roads on the fringes of London to ease traffic congestion on the approaches to the capital. It was during the war years that the Road Board came up with schemes for the Great West Road, a new North Circular Road and Western Avenue.

There was a great deal of confused thought about what the new roads were really for, particularly in the case of Western Avenue, which was to run from the built-up area out into open country. Such roads could by-pass congested routes into London, but they would also lead into areas that would become ripe for development. As they were to be built mostly through open country, they could be properly planned and made wide enough for modern traffic conditions. Of Western Avenue the eminent planner Colin Buchanan has noted: 'There was, in fact, complete confusion as to the road's function, whether it was to be a traffic artery or a development road, and such confusion was to bedevil road planning for the next twenty years.'

When the road building actually began after the First World War, encouraged in the 1920s by extra finance provided by schemes to reduce unemployment, it provided around the western, northern and eastern fringes of London a web-like structure of new avenues which became the focus of

The first few yards of the Great West Road under construction. At the Brentford end, one or two houses were demolished for the new road, but for most of its length it ran out into open country. Government funds to help relieve unemployment provided much of the money for arterial roads

rapid, unplanned development. And in West Middlesex the opening of Western Avenue, the Great West Road and the linking North Circular Road was an added impetus to the development of what was to become the single greatest concentration of industry in the country, running from Wembley through Park Royal south and west to Twickenham.

By the mid-1930s, the new roads were bustling with motorized transport, carrying goods from show piece factories into London and to other parts of the country. The most spectacular of the new avenues was undoubtedly the Great West Road, which had been officially opened by King George V in 1925. It had begun as a by-pass for Brentford, where traffic congestion in the narrow high street had been regarded as a problem since the middle of the nineteenth century. The coming of the electric tram in 1901, hogging the middle of the road, had been the final straw, and the act to build the new road had actually been passed in 1914, but was delayed by the war. The official programme of the opening suggested that the new road was the most spectacular highway achievement since Roman times: it was laid out in a clean curve running from the fringes of Brentford into open country, with space alongside the carriage way for the laying of mains gas, electricity and water pipes.

One of the first firms to find a site here was Smiths Crisps, which moved out from Cricklewood in 1927. There followed a succession of new factories, such as Isleworth Winery, Macleans Ltd, makers of toothpaste and stomach powders, Trico-Folbert, a British subsidiary of the American car windscreen manufacturers, Firestone tyres, Curry's cycles and radios, and Gillette UK Ltd, the American safety razor manufacturers.

In time, this stretch of the Great West Road close to the London exit became known as 'the Golden Mile' and even today, when it has developed a

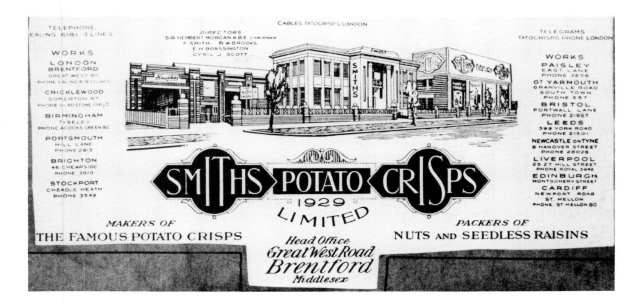

somewhat forlorn air, it is still possible to imagine how strangely gleaming and futuristic it must have looked to the motorist of the 1930s. It became a kind of roadside gallery of modern architecture as each firm used the aspect of its site to project a brand new image to the world. American firms, in particular, favoured this stretch of road, and it was estimated that about sixty per cent of those which set up in Britain between the wars came here. Infected by the style of the area, British firms liked to trumpet the splendour. In 1936, Curry's journal proclaimed:

Above: Smiths Crisps was one of the first firms to colonize the Great West Road, when they moved from Cricklewood to a brand new factory in the mid-1920s. The modern factories which lined arterial roads mostly manufactured for the growing consumer market

Below: Another classic, showpiece factory on the Great West Road, Macleans

It is a worthy home for our great national concern. Its publicity power must be incalcuable. Well might Mr Albert Curry suggest that perhaps the advertising department should contribute £1000 per annum for such astounding publicity value!

It is indeed true that nowhere in the whole of the British Isles is there a road which will advertise Curry's to the world as the Great West Road. . . .

Have you seen this building by night? It's worth motoring many miles to see. Curry's on the front: Curry's on the tower; Cycles and Radio on the tower, all ablaze with vivid Neon lighting; and the whole front flood-lit with glorious intensity – a really marvellous spectacle.

It was in daylight, at the start of his travels for *English Journey* in 1934, that J.B. Priestley took in the spectacle from one of the new motor-coaches which were now competing with railways on long-distance routes, and he could hardly believe his eyes:

After the familiar muddle of West London, the Great West Road looked very odd. Being new, it did not look English. We might suddenly have rolled into California. Or, for that matter, into one of the main avenues of the old exhibitions like the Franco-British Exhibition [at the White City] of my boyhood. These decorative little buildings, all glass and concrete and chromium plate, seem to my barbaric mind to be merely playing at being factories.

The new factories were certainly quite unlike those of Priestley's Victorian Northern England, but in the context of London manufacturing they were in fact a natural extension of an old tradition of the capital making things chiefly for its own consumer market. What was new was its style, its use of new technology, and its concentration on the products of rising mass consumerism. On the Wembley Exhibition site in the 1930s you would find,

The illuminated Hudson Motors limousine, complete with dummy occupants, was part of the exciting night-time display along the Great West Road in the 1930s

for example, Claude-General Neon Lights Ltd in the shell of the South Africa Pavilion, Modern Kitchen Equipments Ltd in the old India Pavilion, and the Expanded Rubber Company Ltd in what had been the Palace of Arts. Here, and in the area around, were gathered a host of mostly small-scale manufacturing concerns, many of which had been established in and then had moved out of inner London, others of which were brand new. The same thing had occurred all the way around the North Circular Road and in Park Royal; printers, coach builders, radio works, cosmetic manufacturers, metal goods factories had established themselves.

In the 1930s, there was a sizeable motor industry in the Park Royal area. This is the Hudson Motors body shop in their factory at the junction of the Great West Road and the North Circular Road. Many coachbuilders moved out from the West End to West Middlesex in the inter-war years and made cars rather than horse-drawn carriages

It is doubtful whether much of this expansion could have taken place without the development of electricity, which freed old industries from dependence on steam and mechanical power and gave them much greater flexibility in their sites. Nor would the distribution of the goods have been nearly so convenient without motor lorries and new roads. And the whole edifice of this new consumer society required new breeds of men and women to run it, and to sell its goods.

ON THE roads, the lorry driver began to replace the cabman with his horse-drawn vehicle. In 1921, there were 49,000 cabmen – twice as many as there were lorry drivers. But by 1931, the number of goods vehicle drivers overall had increased from 73,000 to 86,000, and the motor men represented a clear majority – 49,000. The foundation of the motor road haulage business was laid when the government sold off cheaply army surplus lorries after the Great War. Many of the ex-servicemen who had learned to drive them in the forces became lorry drivers. Firms which had fleets of horse-drawn vehicles had to

An early motor lorry, with solid wheels, drawn up outside one of the most celebrated Great West Road factories of Firestone, the American tyre company. This Horlicks tanker was having its wheels changed: it drove out with a set of Firestone inflatable tyres

retrain the cabmen, used to a slow and pungent routine of reins and harness, straw and oats. According to *The New Survey of London Life and Labour* it usually took a cabman six weeks' fairly constant teaching before he could drive a motor with any confidence. It was quite a different routine!

A horse shares the cabman's knowledge of routes frequently traversed, and often leads the way, moving at a steady speed of about seven miles an hour. On the other hand, motors need constant control and move three or four times as fast as the horse. The cabman turned motor driver at first forgot that he had to steer all the time, and was a bad judge of short distances in manoeuvring his vehicle.

Primitive motor vehicles, long journeys and overnight stops in the truck or in the new cafés and lodging houses which sprang up along the trunk roads made lorry driving in the early days demanding, exciting and somewhat disreputable. Bill Taylor, who drove long distance in the 1920s and 30s, needed more than a little resourcefulness to get by.

I couldn't read or write, so when a firm gave me a delivery note, they used to give the orders of a night-time for the following morning. So I'd take the notes home and try and work out a route which I was going to do, using a map. I'd look on the map for names of places that were the same as those on my delivery notes. I'd make a line right the way across the map, say, from Holloway right up to Barnet and up on the North Road to Darlington or, say, York, and each big town I was going through I'd mark on the map. So, when I pulled up at that town I'd get the map out and ask people which was the best way to the next town I'd marked. This was how I got on. I went from one town to another asking which way because I couldn't read any of the signs on the road. It was easier in this way on the horses, because some of them knew where they were going. The horse used to help a lot, but when it changed to motors I had to do it all myself, and I had to use these tricks to get me through.

Driving was very different in those days. You had two half windscreens up the front, and if the rain was coming down you'd turn the top half up so that you could see, but the rain would come through the gap and you'd get wet. And we had a little hand operated windscreen wiper which you could use every now and again. And you had nothing round the sides on the model 'T' Ford and if it rained you had this sheeting that you used to tie up, so you could just see over the top, but your face still got wet.

The joy was the open road, going to different places, meeting different people. Of course, you met so many up North who spoke different to you. And you were your own boss, you could do what you wanted. Once you left the firm you were your own guv'nor.

As long as I was behind the wheel driving, I was happy. And when I used to go away on journey work, I'd perhaps be away a week at a time and we used to have to sleep rough in the lorry because often the guv'nor had no money. I've come home lousy, white lice running in my jersey, that's how bad it was in those days. You slept under canvas to keep you warm in the back of the lorry. And there used to be these lorry girls in the cafés, and they'd clean your lorry for a few bob, and you'd take them from one town to another. Sometimes they'd stop with you a whole week, sleep with you and keep you company. This is the way they lived. Sometimes you'd give them a lunch or kept them in grub and cigarettes. When the wives found out about these lorry girls, that used to break their marriages up.

In the new factories themselves, a very large number of single women were employed on routine, sometimes soul-destroying work under an extremely strict regime. Lateness, talking on the job and untidiness could easily lead to dismissal. Some of these women, like Edie Bedding, left the old West End cottage industries which had in the past serviced the aristocratic Season but which were now shrinking, to look for better and regular money on the factory floor.

I was at a private little firm, doing dressmaking in the West End. There was only four of us, and we made hand-made things for well-to-do people – a lot of outfits for weddings, like lady's suitings. I liked the work very much

A primitive production line at the Heinz factory in Park Royal in 1930. Heinz moved to its new, green-field site, in 1925; a pioneer of the new industrial belt which grew up there

but it was seasonal, you were working from September to January, then they put you off until May.

I went to a dance and I met some girls who were working for Heinz, and they said what a good firm it was and they said 'oh, you could come to our place, the money's good and the girls are ever so friendly, you'll like it there'. I told my parents about it, but they didn't like it. They'd seen the girls from the Fullers chocolate factory in Hammersmith Broadway and they looked messy. They had chocolate all over them when they came out, and they used to go down the local pub at lunchtime.

Well, I kept on and I got my own way in the end. But to start with I didn't like it at all. When I went to Heinz my job was sorting beans. When these beans came along on the conveyor belt, they were coming along ever so thick, you just had to turn them ever so lightly with your hand, just to make sure there were no black ones in there, and there was a small container where you dropped the black beans. But you didn't have many to put in there because the beans were so perfect anyway. And I was doing this for eight hours a day, sitting by the belt watching these beans go past, and it used to almost send me to sleep staring at them, because we weren't allowed to talk at all, we had to get on with our work.

At the really sharp end of the new consumerism was the door-to-door salesman, a much less respected figure than the commercial traveller who dealt with tradesmen and was better paid. Many of them sold vacuum cleaners. But the vacuum cleaner, the electrically-powered symbol of suburban, labour-saving housewifery, was not taken up as enthusiastically as one might have expected in the inter-war years. Electricity was expensive, and it took time for people to get used to the idea that this new gadget could actually be worth the expense. It was therefore quite a task for vacuum cleaner manufacturers, like the American firm Hoover, to convert the London householder to their machines. But Hoover brought with them from America the aggressive sales pitch of the new industry, building themselves a show piece factory on Western Avenue in 1932, which today is the subject of a preservation order. And the company drilled the door-to-door salesman, who carried the vacuum cleaner to the customer, in high-pressure sales techniques and unquestioning loyalty to the product. By all accounts he had a thankless if sometimes amusing job, as Sam Tobin, whose patch was Arnos Grove, Enfield and Palmers Green in the late 1930s, remembers:

You knocked on the door. 'Good morning madam I represent the North Metropolitan Electric Power Supply Company' – that was the authority in the area prior to nationalization. 'I have been sent along because you are entitled to have one of your carpets and some of your furniture cleaned with the latest Hoover vacuum machine.' Very often it would be 'not today thank you', but if you got inside you would follow a script almost down to the last letter that they taught you in a training course. I laid out the Kapok, I laid out the sand in strips, and I laid out the saltpetre, plugged in the Hoover and cleaned them up, trying to charm and persuade the housewife all the while. And whatever objection they had, you were taught an answer to it. They might say, 'oh my husband wouldn't like me to get involved in buying one of these', and I would say 'now I see you've got a very nice lawn. No doubt your husband has one of these cylinder machines that he cuts the grass with. Not using the old shears method is he?'

Hoover vacuum cleaners leaving the Prince's Road workshop en route to the dealer and customer. The Hoover jingle, still in use today, is reproduced on the side of the van

It could be pretty soul-destroying though, because you could go for weeks without a sale, and if it was bad weather or if Electrolux or newspaper subscription salesmen had done your territory, it was very difficult to get a demonstration anywhere. You had to survive on the £2 a week retainer they gave you, and even when you made a sale, your commission, say £3 for a Hoover Senior, was taken off your retainer, so you only ended up being £1 better off. So to encourage the salesmen, and to put the spirit of the firm in their hearts, sort of thing, the Company would have these sing songs and some salesmen used to sing them in the storerooms before they went out on the road on Monday mornings. They would be standard popular tunes of the day, with Hoover words. (This verse was sung to the tune of the American military ditty, 'The Caissons go rolling along'.)

> All the dirt, all the grit,
> Hoover gets it every bit,
> For it beats as it sweeps as it cleans.
> It deserves all its fame, for it backs up every claim,
> For it beats as it sweeps as it cleans.
>
> Oh it's hi-hi-hee, the kinds of dirt are three,
> We tell the world just what it means,
> Bing bing bing, Spring or Fall,
> The Hoover gets 'em all,
> For it beats as it sweeps as it cleans.

By the late 1930s, something like forty per cent of households owned a Hoover, and though the consumer revolution in Britain was not in full swing until after the Second World War, it was during this decade that much of the groundwork was laid. American-style advertising was then established and the Victorian industry shaken up by newcomers from across the Atlantic.

In one field in particular, it was the American advertising agencies, such as J. Walter Thompson who arrived in London in 1919, that stole the march on their established British counter-parts, and that was in radio. In America, commercial radio was accepted early on, and the sponsored programme had become a feature of life from the 1920s. Britain was typically much more cautious, first resisting the spread of radio and then allowing five major radio manufacturers to form the British Broadcasting Company in 1922. Visits by Lord Reith and others to America led swiftly to a political decision not to allow in commercial radio. National newspapers, fearful for their advertising revenue, were also hostile. The British Broadcasting Corporation, surviving on Post Office licences rather than advertising, was established in 1927.

A couple of sponsored broadcasts had been transmitted before 1927. Harrods tried it as early as 1923, and Selfridge – always in the forefront of new ideas – organized a fashion talk from the Eiffel Tower in 1925. The formation of the BBC two years later was supposed to put an end to commercial radio in Britain, but the pressure for a new advertising medium was such that a way was found to foil the government's monopolistic system.

A few enterprising individuals, notably Captain L.F. Plugge, set up stations on the Continent and began to broadcast sponsored programmes to England. Plugge founded Radio Normandy in 1930, and over the next few years Athlone, Hilversum, Madrid and Toulouse (evocative names from the dials of thirties radios) all had a go at beaming advertising into Britain. However, the most successful and best known station was Luxembourg.

The British Press behaved as if Radio Luxembourg and the other stations did not exist, never mentioning them or publishing programme information, and putting pressure on established British advertising agencies to ignore them. But American concerns, like J. Walter Thompson, persuaded their clients to give radio a try, and before long the commercial radio stations were carrying advertisements for Lifebouy toilet soap, Rinso, Palmolive, Ford Motor Company, Colgate dental cream and so on.

J. Walter Thompson, who moved into Bush House in 1922, converted the swimming pool in the basement into a sound studio, and recorded up to forty-four different sponsored programmes every week for Radio Luxembourg. Londoners tuned in, and surveys suggest that there was a very large listening public in the 1930s, some of whom could be heard humming jingles like the 'We are the Ovaltineys' song as they went about their daily work.

At the same time another powerful American influence had invaded the capital: the cinema. There were already about ninety cinemas in London before the First World War, and an embryo British industry had been established which competed with the American imports. But the war wiped out British cinema, and in the 1920s it was Hollywood which completely dominated the market. This became the subject of great national concern, not least because it was felt that the diet of American movies was advertising American products and undermining British industry. A block was put on the showing of imported films by the Cinematographic Films Act of 1927, which required cinemas to show a quota of British films.

Though many of the British films subsequently produced were regarded as second-rate 'quota quickies', the act did allow a considerable industry to grow up before the Second World War. Inevitably it became established around London, characteristically on the fringes of the new industrial zone, but also in the more run-down of the Victorian suburbs, which were becoming increasingly industrialized in this period. Film studios were set up in Elstree, Croydon, Denham, Surbiton, Pinewood, Cricklewood, Ealing, Fulham and many other places within Greater London. They all worked on electric power, of course, and provide perhaps the most vivid illustration of the fact that this new form of energy enabled industry to set up more or less wherever it liked, and most of it liked London.

Sir Alexander Korda's Denham Studios in Buckinghamshire, built in 1936, had their own power plant, but most used public supplies which by then were much better organized. London's great attraction for the film industry was that it remained the great cultural centre of Britain, and West End actors found it convenient to dash from the studio to the theatre as they enjoyed the employment of both the old and new industries.

A great deal of the new industrial development around London was related to its traditional manufacture: coach builders of the horse-drawn era moving

A traffic roundabout at Gants Hill on Eastern Avenue – one of the new, inter-war arterial roads – in 1933. It looks luxuriously spacious, but the colonization of these new roads by 'ribbon development' of houses and factories soon caused problems

to Park Royal to make the bodies of motor vehicles, which would then be displayed in gleaming showrooms in Regent Street, Piccadilly and Mayfair. The consumer society greatly expanded the scale of production and the size of the market, but industry still clung to London.

In fact, the extraordinary story of the rise of the Western industrial belt was extended via the North Circular Road and new arterial roads, such as Eastern Avenue, right around the north of London to the Lea Valley in the east. A great deal of this, so evocative of the 1930s, still survives in buildings of brick with metal-framed windows, a kind of miniature grandeur which to us today looks so tatty and uninspiring.

For the most part, the East End, London's principal industrial zone of the second half of the nineteenth century, did not share this new prosperity. But there is one, gigantic and in many ways anomalous exception – the Ford Motor factory at Dagenham in Essex. Ford was operating in Britain before 1914, and had built his original factory in Old Trafford, Manchester. But in the 1920s, Ford wanted to establish a European base and after a good deal of argument decided on a site near London, against the advice of his leading English representative who had marked out a part of Southampton's dockland. Exactly why Ford went to Dagenham to build his monster production works is not clear, but the lure of London for Americans was clearly very influential. The great complex was built on marshy land by the Thames and supported on enormous concrete piles. It had its own foundry and during the 1930s the furnace was fuelled partly by LCC rubbish which had formerly been dumped on the site. Nearby was a mass of unskilled labour, which had also been recently 'exported' from inner London to live on the vast Becontree 'cottage' estate (see Chapter Four).

However, Ford's move southwards was an unusual episode in the story of London's prosperity in the inter-war years. Most of the industry which grew up in the new industrial belt was either entirely new, and related to electrically powered manufacture, or had moved out from the centre in order to find space. Very few industries arrived from the North: it was the people, not the factories, who made the great migration to the capital.

CHAPTER THREE

THE HEYDAY OF LONDON TRANSPORT

THE NEAT design of the map of London's Underground railways, with the yellow Circle Line bisected by a red Central Line, from which radiate brown, black and blue lines, is so familiar and so established that it looks as if at some time in the past the tubes must have been carefully planned. Who was responsible for the creation of the Underground and why, few people know, but they imagine it must have been some early incarnation of what everybody calls London Transport: the authority responsible for the fact that tube trains break down, fares rise and fall, buses travel around town in convoy and keep people waiting at bus stops. Life before London Transport is either unknown or largely forgotten, and all the difficulties people have in getting about the capital are blamed on the failings of a public authority which always appears to be in a sorry state administratively and financially.

It might come as a surprise, therefore, to the gloomy commuter waiting for the lift to ascend to ground level on, say, the Northern Line at Belsize Park Station to learn that this was the creation in 1907 of a private company headed by an extraordinary American financier called Charles Tyson Yerkes. And how many hurrying travellers have noticed that at Oxford Circus two stations have been welded into one? From the street, the original stop on the Central Line, opened in 1900, can still be seen alongside the Yerkes station, with its familiar 'ox-liver' tiling of 1906. Both these were built by private enterprise, which is responsible indirectly for the fact that passengers on the old tube lines are sometimes flung about as the train negotiates a tight corner into a station. The cheapest routes lay under roads because no 'easement' had to be paid to the owners of buildings above, so that Underground companies burrowed round corners to follow a bend; your electric Underground carriage is probably following a route established long before the Great War by horse-drawn traffic!

The truth of the matter is that what survives of London Transport today was largely the creation of private enterprise before 1933, the year in which the capital's tubes, trams and buses were first put in charge of a public authority. And the shape and extent of the system was dictated by the pursuit of profit, often with very disappointing results for investors. The Underground map everyone knows is, in fact, a very clever distortion of the *actual* route the capital tubes take, and seeks to make some logical sense out of a network of tunnels and tracks which were never planned as a system but came about by the piecemeal efforts of a number of railway promoters.

Although the commercial nature of London Transport before 1933 produced a rather haphazard system, it was also in many ways a very vigorous operation and by use of new sources of power – electricity and petrol – which became available around 1900, laid the foundations for what might be called the heyday of public transport in the capital in the late 1930s. For between 1914 and 1939 Londoners used buses, tubes, trams and trolley buses much

Previous pages: Park Royal tube station on the Piccadilly Line extension in 1936. It was designed by the architect Charles Holden, who gave the Underground much of its style in the inter-war years

more than they had done ever before, or have since. Though motor cars were already contributing to serious traffic jams in the 1930s, few Londoners in this period owned a car and they therefore spent much more of their money travelling for work or pleasure.

A survey of the rides per head of population in London shows the extraordinary increase in travel. For tubes, buses and trams the average Londoner took 210 rides a year in 1911 and 388 in 1938–9; if railways are included, the increase is from 250 to 443. The absolute highpoint was 1949 when the private car gradually began to take passengers away from public transport.

Private transport operators, particularly the Underground Group, made great efforts to improve transport, but it is a mistake to imagine that the commuter of the 1920s or 1930s had a much easier time of it than his or her successor today. For one of the reasons for the increase in travel was that from the 1890s right through to the inter-war period a host of social and economic changes fundamentally altered the pattern of journeys between home and work in London.

Before the Great War, London already had a great army of commuters who travelled to work by train, tube, tram and bus. Cheap workmen's fares, introduced from the 1860s to compensate the poor for the destruction of housing involved in much railway building, had allowed hundreds of thousands

A traffic jam in Regent Street in 1929. At first motor cars and buses seemed to ease traffic problems because they were faster and more compact than horse-drawn vehicles. But as their numbers rapidly increased, they choked the old road network in the centre

of the lower paid clerks and artisans to live in modest, terraced suburbs, particularly in the north-east of London as the railway company operating there had the lowest fare policy. The war itself had a profound effect on the nature of travel in London, however. In answer to the demands of munition workers the government froze rents, and this discouraged movement from one home to another as people remained where they were to benefit from rent control. At the same time, the rise of armament factories, many of them set up on the fringes of London, altered the distribution of jobs. As a result, the amount of travel increased enormously between 1914 and 1918.

After the war, the trends of industrial development continued to pull homes and workplace apart: the LCC was building enormous 'cottage' council estates in places like Becontree in the east, while much of the new employment was growing in the west. Despite the continuation of workmen's fares on the railways and trams (they were never available on buses) the cost and inconvenience of travel was considerable and the cause of a great deal of concern. The physical and mental distress of commuting was a lively issue. So, even though many people gained through an inter-war reduction in working hours – the eight-hour day became more and more common – they had to spend much more time travelling to and from work. Moreover, the traveller could only get a cheap workman's ticket up to 8.00 a.m. – if he missed that train, he paid more. So often, in order to save on fares, people would arrive in London far earlier than they needed, having been jam-packed into the early morning cheap train. George Matthews was one of those who experienced the commuter crushes of the 1930s as he tried to board the train from Eltham:

> When you got to the station it was like a football match, absolutely solid packed with people. To get a workman's ticket, you see, you had to arrive in central London by eight o'clock, so you had to catch the 7.36 train. Everyone wanted to catch it. Because a lot of us on those new estates didn't have any money to spare (we were all paying for our houses) you'd even find people who didn't start work till nine or ten o'clock, clerical-type people, they would all catch that last workman's train as well to get the cheap fare.
>
> And even when it arrived, it was practically full-up with people travelling in from Dartford, so we'd be waiting on the platform four or five lines deep, and so people opened the doors to get in, you'd have two or three blokes nearly falling out. It was really unpleasant, everybody would be shoving, pushing, there would be shouting, elbowing, near fighting sometimes; oh, it was absolutely murder. Sometimes you couldn't get on, but even when you did, you'd stand all the way, about twenty of you in a compartment meant for eight.

George was one of the many people who eventually turned to pedal power as the cheapest, most efficient and most enjoyable way of getting to and from work. Though cycling was never a statistically substantial part of commuting, it was a popular option for many poorer paid workers and there would be great armadas of bicycles along roads bordered by factories at clocking-in and out times. It's estimated there were two million cyclists in the London area in 1936. Some of the cyclists, like Les White, travelled quite extraordinary distances every day, and they developed ways and means of making the journey as painless as possible.

I used to live in Bow, and I worked at Hoover's in Perivale, which is some seventeen miles away, and this journey I used to do by cycle. I'd be on my bike doing thirty-two or sometimes forty miles a day – thought nothing of it.

I started work at seven o'clock in the morning, which meant I had to leave home at about a quarter past five. When I got to Aldgate I used to meet my friend from West Ham and we'd cycle together most mornings, side by side, chatting about all sorts of things, the weather, football, family – it helped pass the time. We had a few dodges as well to get to work more quickly, because if you were late at Hoover's, they locked you out. Oxford Street was full of traffic lights and we used to get to know these lights quite well travelling morning after morning, and being early morning there was little traffic about, so you could see almost the whole length of Oxford Street, all the traffic lights from one end to the other. So we worked it out that, if you caught one light, if you pedalled like mad, you'd be able to catch the next seven lights without stopping – they'd all be green. We got expert at that.

Another thing we did, was to get lifts. If a market lorry or a cart was going our way we'd reach out and grab the tailboard and get a pull-along for as long as possible, it might be a couple of miles, or just fifty yards, it depended how lucky you were.

Because many employers had strict regulations about punctuality, some of them locking out late workers, the dash to get to work on time put even more of a strain on those travelling in from the new estates. For some, like Doris Hanslow, this daily ordeal was too much, after she had moved from Bermondsey – where she could walk to work – to the LCC Downham estate, on London's suburban fringe.

From our house I used to walk over a mile to the tram stop and get the workman's tram into London. It was terrible walking across the half-built estate, it got really muddy in the winter; but what was the worst was the tram itself. You'd be herded on, packed tight together, then you'd sway and sway with the tram, and I'd feel sick and no end of times I'd have to get off because I couldn't take the journey – I'd actually be sick. Sometimes a kind conductor would let you stand out the front and get some air; then it was alright.

That journey took about twenty or thirty minutes and if the tram was late you'd have to run the half a mile to the factory because, if you weren't there dead on eight o'clock, the gates were shut and you was locked out for the morning. So, sometimes you used to wander about till dinner time or go to a friend's house, then you'd go back to work in the afternoon, but you'd lose your money.

Hanging room only on a London
tram in 1919 as commuters battle
home from the Embankment. This
photograph was taken at the time of
a rail strike – which obviously made
things worse – but the tremendous
increase in travel by public transport
between the wars put a great strain
on services

Well, one day, I was so hot, I'd run to get there and just made it in time,
and I just wanted to sit down and get my coat off and sit comfortable, and I
was still shaking from the running, and the forelady, I didn't like her, she
started saying, 'Come on – move!' I thought, 'Well, I can't take no more'
and I just stood up, collected all my things and said 'I'm going home' and
walked out. I just couldn't do it any more and I thought 'Thank God I won't
have to get on that tram and go down there and face that again'.

The widening distance between home and work led to a boom in restaurant
catering, which in turn had the effect of increasing the number of people using
public transport. Many women chose to become waitresses rather than
domestic servants, which meant that they themselves now travelled to work.
And quite a number of firms, anxious to keep up with the times and to cope

with the problem of staff who travelled long distances, brought in canteens – an innovation encouraged by the First World War.

At the same time, transport companies, notably the most powerful of them, the Underground Group, made a deliberate effort to extend the frontiers of the capital in their never-ending search for new passengers. They were able to pursue a policy of colonizing new areas of countryside because London's population, swelled by immigration from the depressed areas of Britain, continued to grow, rising by 1½ million between the wars. While 'inner London' lost population, the new suburbs expanded rapidly. The problem of the commercial companies, which ran the buses and tubes, was to generate enough traffic to repay the enormous capital investment involved in building new lines and modernizing old ones, and they did so by encouraging suburban development and the use of the transport system outside the commuting 'rush hours'. It was a policy which carried over into the era of public ownership of London Transport, for the same people who ran the single most influential company in London dominated the Passenger Transport Board of 1933. This transport imperialism came to an end with the beginnings of a Green Belt policy – designed to prevent more suburban building on the outskirts of the capital – and finally with the outbreak of the Second World War.

The crucial technological revolution in London's transport system took place before the First World War. In the nineteenth century, Londoners were taken to and from work and about town on steam railways and in horse-drawn vehicles. In the heart of the capital, the West End, the horse bus held sway as the horse tram – a working- and lower-middle-class form of transport – had been banned in the 1860s. Trams ran from the boundaries of the central area out to places like Camberwell, Peckham and Archway, providing a service which was cheap and invaluable to those who lived in the new suburbs of terraced houses. London's steam-driven Underground went around the central area, linking up the mainline railway stations, which, like the tram, had been kept out of the West End.

The first break with this pattern of transport came with the building of the 'deep level' tube, using a technique for burrowing below the surface of the capital's streets which had been perfected in the boring of tunnels under the Thames. The blue clay sub-soil proved ideal for this and the first Underground railway proper of this type was the line from Stockwell to King William Street in the City in 1890. All previous Underground lines had been built using the 'cut and cover' method, which involved demolishing a whole lot of property, digging a large trench, and filling it over again. Steam trains were, anyway, quite unsuited to deep tunnels as ventilation was a serious problem. Lines running near the surface had to have frequent open cuttings.

In fact, the initial plan for this first tube railway (the City & South London) when it was being tunnelled in the 1880s was to use cable power to pull the trains. But during the time it was being built, the technological problems of using electricity to power trams was solved. Railed transport had proved a significant factor in United States cities in the second half of the nineteenth century because roads there were so bad that horse-drawn, carriage-wheel vehicles had only a limited use. The wide open spaces of the New World were moreover ideal for experimentation with electric power carried in an unsightly fashion on overhead wires supported by poles: something the big city authorities in New York and London were not keen on.

American horse tramways were rapidly electrified in the late nineteenth century, and the opportunity to experiment, as well as the great demand for new equipment, gave the Americans a vital lead in developing this new form of traction. The Germans, too, were quick to develop electric power and, in fact, had provided the world's first passenger electric train in Berlin in 1881. In Britain, a seafront electric train in Brighton was opened in 1883 and an electric tramway system in Blackpool in 1885. Electric power had therefore arrived just in time for the City & South London, which in fact installed equipment of a British make – a rarity in the early days of the Underground.

London's second electric tube was the Waterloo & City Line, built in 1898 and early dubbed 'The Drain'. It was significantly a project promoted by a mainline railway company, the London & South Eastern, which wanted a way of getting its passengers direct from Waterloo to what was then still the central goal of the commuter, the City. A spate of tube proposals came up in the 1890s at a time when London's population was rising rapidly and its old horse-drawn and steam-driven transport system was creaking under the weight of travel to and from the centre. Four main schemes emerged in these years, three of them supported by mainline railway companies: the Baker Street to Waterloo; the Great Northern & City Railway from Finsbury Park to Moorgate; and 'The Drain', which was the first to be built. There was one other proposal for a line from Hampstead to Charing Cross, with a branch off to Kings Cross.

Yet another line had been authorized by Parliament in 1891, and this was to prove the most successful of the pioneers. This was the Central London Railway to run from Shepherd's Bush to the Bank. In a period when the financial success of tube lines was in some doubt – the City & South London was not paying much of a return – this Central Line was the best bet. It traced underground the heaviest flow of horse-drawn traffic in the capital from the Bank alongside Cheapside, through Holborn and Oxford Street to the Bayswater Road and finally to Shepherd's Bush. The density of horse-drawn traffic on the roads was, at this time, a good guide to the potential profit of a tube line beneath them.

The basic technical problems of building these lines and providing electric power had been solved. The stumbling block that remained was how to convince investors it was worth putting money into railways which required an enormous capital outlay, but often gave little back. International support was found for the Central Line from investors in Paris, Hamburg, Frankfurt, Berlin and New York, as well as from Britain; and with its equipment supplied by General Electric of America, the first section began to operate in 1900. It had a flat fare of 2d and was quickly dubbed the 'Twopenny Tube'.

But the other schemes were floundering for lack of finance: part of the line from Baker Street to Waterloo had been burrowed out, but the company behind it went bust. It was at this point that an extraordinary figure appeared on the London scene: Charles Tyson Yerkes, a capitalist and speculator from America. Yerkes was in his sixties and had a very murky past as an operator in

A portrait of the remarkable American, Charles Tyson Yerkes, who was responsible for the financing of three London tube lines, the Bakerloo, Piccadilly and Hampstead (now Northern). While British investors were cautious about putting money into tubes, Yerkes persuaded Americans they could make a killing out of the London commuter

the corrupt American finance scene of the late nineteenth century. His speciality was over-valuing some pretty shoddy assets, including tramway systems, and he is reported as describing his line of business as 'to buy up old junk, fix it up a little and unload it upon other fellows'. In America he had spent a few months in jail for his shady dealings. But, as far as American investors were concerned, he had a good track record in building the elevated railway – 'the EL' – in Chicago.

Yerkes was, in retrospect, the ideal man for London's Underground railways, in the sense that he had a gift for persuading people to put their money into something which was not really profitable. He proceeded to do so by buying himself into the District Railway, which was in financial trouble, as well as the proposed Hampstead tube and other lines. This was a period in history, as we have seen in earlier chapters, when American financiers were particularly keen to break into the London scene. Yerkes clearly thought he could make a killing in London, though he told a Commons committee: 'I have got to a time when I am not compelled to go into this business, but seeing the way things are in London, I made up my mind that this would be my last effort.' And it was, for he died in December 1905 before any of the schemes he masterminded were completed.

In the few years he was in London, Yerkes and his associates laid the foundations for the underground system we know today. By bringing together the management of a number of tube lines, the District, Bakerloo, Piccadilly and Hampstead, a basis was formed out of which the great combine, the Underground Group, grew. And he brought to London an unmistakable American flavour and drive which survived after his death, thanks to the American managers and experts he and his successors imported.

Proposals for new tube lines were being put forward all the time in the early 1900s, prompted by the success of the Central Line, and Yerkes and his associates had to fight off a challenge from another group of American financiers headed by J. Pierpont Morgan. The ins and outs of this battle are too complex and subtle to go into here, but what they amounted to was an attempt by two groups of tube railway backers to convince Parliamentary committees that the lines they proposed were worthwhile, that they would do a decent job, and that they had the money to complete their schemes. The Morgan Group had teamed up with a tramway company and was proposing, amongst other tube lines, one which would run through north-east London. By a bit of sharp dealing, in which his company got a controlling interest in one of the Morgan company associates, Yerkes undermined their opposition and emerged as the victor, scuppering the proposed North East London Line and allowing his undertakings a clear field for developing the Bakerloo, Piccadilly and Hampstead lines.

In America it had become the practice of tramway promoters to build out into open country, well beyond city boundaries, and to make a killing on increased land prices when housing was put up around the tramway stops. They often opened amusement parks at the end of the line to encourage traffic. If you provided the transport, housing would surely follow. For the most part, the London tube schemes had not reflected this policy. They simply attempted to provide a new form of urban transport, which would cream off traffic within the existing congested built-up area. This was the case with the original scheme for the Hampstead tube, but when Yerkes came in, he quickly proposed that the line should be extended into the undeveloped fields of North London at Golders Green.

The story goes that Yerkes took a carriage to the top of Hampstead Heath with a colleague, who had earlier been sent out to scout along the route. Stepping out of the carriage, Yerkes asked: 'Where's London?' It was pointed out to him and he determined there and then to build the railway. He also wanted a station under the Heath, beneath the Bull and Bush Pub, part of which was excavated. But it was abandoned and the terminus established at Golders Green.

In putting the case for the extension of the line to Golders Green, counsel for the Yerkes Group told a committee in 1901: 'It is a very pretty part of the country right away to the North, and a country which is eminently suited for building both the better class of houses and also houses for the labouring classes.'

The American speculators' instinct for extending transport into the countryside was complemented in England by the 'garden city' movement, which grew up in the late nineteenth century in opposition to the Victorian lack of urban planning, and which sought to create a new townscape where housing

was segregated from the industrial heart of the city. At Golders Green, the two impulses came together when, soon after the station was opened in 1907, work began on Hampstead Garden Suburb.

What might be called the 'Yerkes' part of the Underground system – the Bakerloo, Piccadilly and Hampstead lines, as well as the electrification of the District – was completed by 1907. Their characteristic stations, still seen in many parts of London, are faced in deep red, glazed tiles. On the technical and management side, Yerkes brought over to London a team of American engineers who introduced to London a transatlantic railway lingo, including OK and the terms northbound and southbound instead of the English 'Up' and 'Down' for the direction of trains. And prim commentators at the time thought the Americans had encouraged in Underground staff a foreign brashness: letters in *The Times* complained of stations' names being distorted by Cockney accents, Hampstead becoming 'Ampstid' and Highgate 'Igit'.

At the same time as the tube railways were being established, there was a revolution in the capital's surface transport provided by trams, buses and cabs. Tramways were being electrified, making them brighter, cleaner, faster and capable of much longer journeys. And the first motorized buses and cabs were being experimented with on the city streets.

The battle between the American financiers over the tube lines had caused quite a stir and there was a feeling that it was wrong that the planning of London's transport system should be left to competition between capitalists. As the Chairman of a Commons Select Committee said of Yerkes' fight with Morgan, it all seemed to be 'a game in which it was proposed to make the London road pawns on the chequer board of Wall Street'.

There was one authority in London which could reasonably claim to be in a

The wide open spaces of Golders Green, before the arrival of the Hampstead tube line in 1907. It was Yerkes who wanted the line extended to Golders Green, and his belief that it would lead to the development of the area was almost immediately justified

Knightsbridge, one of London's Edwardian tube stations with its 'ox-liver' tiling that indicated it had been built by Yerkes

position to take over and plan the transport system: the London County Council. This had been set up in 1889 and was run for the first few years by 'progressive' liberals, among them Sir John Williams Benn, grandfather of Anthony Wedgwood Benn. Legislation enabled the LCC to purchase and operate the commercial horse tramways, which had been set up in the 1870s, and the progressives were keen to do so and to use this section of the transport system to further their social policies of providing cheaper travel for the working classes from city centre to suburbs. Between 1896 and 1906, the LCC bought the assets of nine tram companies north and south of the river and proceeded to electrify the lines, becoming one of the major transport operators in the capital.

The LCC pressed for a government inquiry into London's transport and hoped that it might be given some overall planning powers as had happened, for example, in New York, where the subway lines were built by the Rapid Transit Commission and run by private companies. Instead of an inquiry, a Royal Commission was set up in 1903 and deliberated for two years. It recommended the creation of a London Traffic Board, but no action was taken. London's transport was left as a most extraordinary jumble, with the LCC and private companies jostling for power and trying to make sense of their own bits of the system.

Electrification of the tramway system therefore came in bit by bit. A group called Imperial Tramways, based in Bristol, teamed up with American associates, bought out an ailing horse tram line in Hammersmith run by West Metropolitan Tramways and created on 4 April 1901 the first permanent public electric tramway in the capital, The London United, which ran from Shepherds Bush to Acton. On the east and south-east sides of London, the local authorities outside the LCC area (which was much smaller than the built-up area of London) took over and built tramways; East Ham running its first electric service in June 1901. The LCC itself was slow to shift to electrification, partly because it lacked technical expertise, but also because it rejected the use of overhead wires for power – acceptable in outer London – and favoured the 'conduit' system, which involved digging up roads to provide the power lines for the trams. It was the Highways Committee of the LCC which got the council started by buying an entire demonstration system of conduit trams from the American Westinghouse firm at an exhibition in the Agricultural Hall, Islington, in June 1900. They even bought the tram driver – motorman in American parlance – and installed him with the system at Camberwell. This began to operate in December 1901.

At this time it was electric traction which appeared to be the thing of the future – the petrol engine was still in its infancy. The Royal Commission on London Traffic concluded that the motor bus was of minor importance, and a tramway manager proclaimed in evidence that 'it is an anachronism and is looked upon more or less as a fit object for a museum and not for public service'. Around the world, there were futuristic schemes for light railways, which many people believed would solve the transport problems of great cities. In 1901, the LCC's tramway manager and engineer went to Boston and New York to look at the shallow subways developed there and came up with the idea for something similar in London.

A great problem with the tramway system in London was that its northern and southern sections were not connected as the lines had never been allowed across the Thames. The LCC planned to solve this by creating a subway tunnel under Kingsway, a grand new avenue created as part of a slum clearance scheme from Aldwych to Holborn. The Kingsway tunnel would link the northern system, ending at Theobalds Road, with that on the other side of the Thames. The tunnel was completed around 1904, but remained unused until the LCC had won permission to run trams along the Embankment and across Westminster Bridge at the end of 1906. Trams crossed Westminster Bridge and Blackfriars Bridge for the first time in 1906 and 1909, and something like an integrated system was beginning to emerge in the centre as the LCC took over the tram system in its own area. But within Greater London the whole thing was fragmented, the boroughs outside the LCC running their own services on the east side of the capital, and private operators running the trams to the west.*

Electric trams were, nevertheless, a great boon to Londoners, as they were cheaper than buses, started earlier and were much more comfortable and better lit than the old horse-drawn vehicles. The murky journey home redolent of the Victorian era was greatly brightened by this innovation. Their heyday came just before the First World War, when competition from their great rival on the roads, the motor bus, was just beginning to take effect.

The Great War put an end temporarily to the challenge of the buses, as so

* The Kingsway subway tunnel was in use until 1951, and the station under the road at Holborn survived until recently as the GLC's flood control centre. The southern part of the tunnel is now an underpass.

many vehicles were commandeered for service at the front. At the same time, troop movements around the capital, the influx of office workers to keep the home front operating, and the travel of munitions workers increased the 'travel habit' in London, and it was in these years that many people became accustomed to tube travel. The trams, too, despite a shortage of men and equipment, were carrying more passengers at the end of the war than at the beginning.

Before the war, there had been some co-operation on fare structures among the competing elements of the transport system and the Underground Group – the biggest owner of Underground railways – had absorbed the London General Omnibus Company and three major tramway companies to become easily the most powerful element in the system. The experience of the war itself, as in so many other aspects of British life, won many people over to the idea that a co-ordinated system was economically and socially better than fierce competition. But the old laissez-faire transport system was still a muddle in 1918.

Its development in the 1920s and 1930s was carried out by three main groups, who had to operate to a considerable extent in their own 'territories'. Perhaps because of its evocative advertising, and the recent nostalgic revival, the best known of these operators is the Metropolitan Railway. Its story is rather unusual in London, in that it was a railway company, operating from a headquarters in Baker Street, which also got involved – through a specially created subsidiary – in the development of its territory for housing. In extending the Metropolitan Line – London's first steam Underground railway – out into the countryside of north-west London in the nineteenth century, it had been forced to buy far more land than it needed for its tracks. It created a surplus land company which got involved in promoting a number of ventures.

One of these, involving a separate Tower Company, with Sir Edward Watkin, the Metropolitan Railway's chairman, at its head, leased land at Wembley Park and attempted to promote an amusement park in the 1880s, with a bigger and better version of the Eiffel Tower as its centrepiece. The Tower in fact remained unfinished and abandoned for many years and was dubbed 'Watkin's Folly'. It was removed to make way for Wembley Stadium in the early 1920s. But the Metropolitan continued to promote development along its lines, and in 1915 adopted the term 'Metroland' for advertising purposes; the origin of the term possibly being a little ditty composed by the journalist, George R. Simms:

> Hearts are light, eyes are brighter,
> In Metroland, Metroland.

Just after the war, the Metropolitan set up a new company, Metropolitan Country Estates Ltd, which acted as a housing developer in places like Pinner and Harrow.

To the south of London, the amalgamation of three railways in 1923 produced a new company, Southern Railways. Some of the lines it took over had already been electrified, but like other mainline railway companies operating in London, much of it was still steam-powered, quite antiquated and unsuitable for short suburban journeys with frequent stops. Southern was exceptional in that it got more of its money from passengers than freight, and it proceeded to carry out a swift electrification of its suburban lines which was virtually complete by the 1930s.

This gave it a huge territory in Kent, Surrey, Sussex and Hampshire which was not invaded by the electric tube, with the exception – and a contentious one as far as Southern Railways were concerned – of the line to Morden which the Underground pushed through in 1928.

The complexity of the rest of the transport system is mind-boggling, with the LCC running the trams in the centre, local authorities such as West Ham or Croydon outside the county area running them in the east and south east, private tramways operating in the west, and a number of bus companies competing for custom in the centre and the 'country' areas around London. But there was one concern which was more powerful than all the others, and in effect set the tone and style of London Transport between the wars.

Lord Ashfield, one of the two great figures in the history of London Transport, with his daughter at the opening of the Morden Line extension in 1924. As Albert Stanley, Ashfield came to London before 1914 to run the tube railway company set up by Yerkes. He became chairman of the London Passenger Transport Board in 1933

Left: One of the famous London Transport posters encouraging people to use the tubes and buses at off-peak hours. For a while, British design flowered under the encouragement and sponsorship of Frank Pick, who wanted to make London Transport the best in the world

Right: A 1938 poster encouraging Londoners to use public transport to enjoy entertainment in the centre of town. It was always difficult to make transport services pay, and posters promoted off-peak travel. By the time this one was on display, London Transport was losing cinema and theatre traffic to the motor car

That anything like a co-ordinated system should have emerged from this muddled situation in the years between 1918 and 1933 is quite remarkable. But it did, and was largely due to the efforts of two men who had joined the Underground Group before the First World War. One was Albert Stanley, later to become Lord Ashfield. He was born in England, but his family emigrated to America, where he became the dynamic manager of a New Jersey tramway company. He was brought over to London in 1908 by the Underground Group, anxious that an American should be in control. The other man was Frank Pick, who joined the Underground Group in 1906, and became their commercial manager in 1912. In terms of style, approach and philosophy, Albert Stanley and Frank Pick created London Transport in the inter-war years and their influence is still evident in the Underground design today.

Between them, Stanley and Pick brought some unity to London's transport system, the one overseeing the expansion of the Underground Group's activities, and the other devising ways of making the whole thing more 'modern', attractive and dynamic.

When the London General Omnibus Company became part of the Underground Group, Frank Pick set off on a kind of walking tour to map out

WEEK-END WALKS

 800 miles of these in London's Country described in 3 books 'Country Walks' 1ST 2ND 3RD series · 3D at station bookstalls

Why wait till later?

new routes for the buses, with the idea that road and tube services should be linked in a supporting system. It was Pick who developed the Underground posters which are collectors' items now. There was a sound commercial reason for these, for the Underground railways suffered from having to provide a 'peak' service for commuters but were under-used outside the rush-hour. Attractive posters urging Londoners to have a day in the country, or a night in town could increase the traffic in off-peak hours. Pick brought in artists such as Graham Sutherland to design these posters and out of his efforts grew a particular genre of British design. During the Great War, he commissioned Edward Johnston to design a new typeface appropriately called 'Underground' for use on the tubes. And Pick experimented with the 'bulls-eye' design for the tube railways, which was to become the familiar London Transport symbol.

As existing tube lines were extended during the inter-war period, and the old stations were modernized to cope with the increase in travel, Pick was able to develop with architects a distinctive style of station design. It is for this reason that so many Londoners imagine that the Underground was essentially a creation of the 1920s and 1930s.

After the Great War there were many proposed extensions of tube lines still outstanding which had been halted by the shift to a war economy. Economic conditions were now quite different; everything was more expensive. Though the Underground Group was anxious to push out into new territory, finding the money proved impossible until, during the first real depression of the inter-war period in 1921, the government offered money for schemes which would relieve unemployment. Lord Ashfield quickly put forward a proposal to claim government finance for the Underground Group. He secured £5 million to build an extension of the Hampstead Line out to Edgware, to modernize existing lines and to create a new junction at Euston.

The Edgware extension, with its neat little stations designed by the Underground Group's architect, S.A. Heaps, laid the foundations for that district's suburban prosperity. The new line was opened to Hendon Station in 1923, and reached Edgware in the following year. One station on the line, Burnt Oak, remained isolated among fields until the LCC began to build its 'cottage' estate of council houses at Watling in 1926. Under the same unemployment scheme (the Trade Facilities Act of 1921) the Hampstead Line was joined with a modernized City & South London tube at Euston and Camden Town, to form the two branches of the present Northern Line. The contractors, Mowlem, brought in Welsh miners to excavate the tunnels for the complex new junction.

Shortly after the Underground Group began work on the extension to Edgware, it pushed southwards into Southern Region mainline railways' territory with the line from Clapham Common to Morden. Once again this was part of an expansionist policy with lines going out into open country in the belief that new traffic would be generated by the creation of suburbs around stations. But pushing tube lines out into open country was a costly gamble, and Lord Ashfield is reported as saying on the opening of the Morden Line that fourteen million passengers a year were needed to make it pay.

In fact, the Underground railways did not pay a respectable return on capital, and one of the major reasons for this was that they faced such fierce competition from electric trams and, particularly in the 1920s, from motor

Right: Workmen blazing the trail on the Underground extension to Morden on the Northern Line in 1924. It is *not* the new line that they are putting down, but a temporary track to bring in materials to build the depot. What the picture does show is how rural the area was before the arrival of the tube

Below: Ten years after it was opened, Morden Station was the centre-piece of a brand new expanse of London's inter-war suburbia. The bus services linked up with the tube to extend London Transport's range and were part of the 'expansionist' policy of the inter-war years

Inset: Morden Station in 1927, a wonderful floodlit expression of the Underground Group's concern with style and taste, and the policy of building stations to entice the public

buses. The Great War had abruptly stopped the rapid development of the motor bus and it took some time to recover. Only 250 were returned to London streets by the War Office after 1918, and the railways and trams at this time carried the great majority of the capital's passengers.

But the bus had always been potentially the most lucrative branch of public transport in the capital, and quickly reasserted itself as new designs were developed making it more comfortable and allowing it to carry more passengers. In fact, within the Underground Group, which owned both buses and tubes, it was the former which paid the dividend. During the Great War, Lord Ashfield had pushed through a 'Common Fund' scheme to which all the branches of London Transport contributed according to a formula based on the ability to pay. The Fund survived the war, and it was the bus service that made the single largest contribution. To some extent this reduced the competition amongst various services, which Ashfield found so wasteful, but the success of the buses in the early 1920s put a strain on the whole system.

Until 1924 there were no authorized bus routes, and independent operators or 'pirates' could compete with the larger companies wherever and whenever they liked. This led to some extraordinary scenes on the busier streets of the capital, as a pirate bus attempted to get ahead of a 'General' while the 'General' buses tried to get either side of the pirate to 'nurse' it away from passengers. There were even stories of pirates doing U turns because there were more passengers waiting on the other side of the road, and conductors jumping from their own bus to a 'General' to rob them of fares. Ted Harrison remembers how the pirates operated quite a different sort of service to the 'Generals':

If you wanted to catch a pirate bus you had to wait at a stop where there was about three people, because if you waited at the stop where there was just one, he'd whizz past and you wouldn't catch him at all. They were just after the crowds of passengers, and if there was a General bus in front they'd want to overtake it. They were speedies, express buses we called them, because no sooner had they stopped than they were away again, you hardly had time to sit down. If you wanted to get anywhere quick, you'd use a pirate, they were good drivers, in and out of the traffic like nobody's business. If they had an accident they never used to wait for the police or anything like that, unless it was serious, but in a smaller accident they'd just pat the bloke on the head and most likely slip him a quid, and away they went. But they were always after the crowds, they'd turn round and go the other way sometimes if they saw a crowd, and come back on a different route, so if you'd got a return you might have to blinking well leg it back.

By 1924 there were about 460 pirate buses operating in London, squeezing the profit margins of the 'General' and other large companies. In that year, bus routes were regulated for the first time, but the pirates continued to compete until the 1930s, hoping to attract passengers by convenient schedules and comfort rather than reduced fares. The peak year for the pirates was 1926 when there were more than 550 on the road, carrying nearly 200 million passengers.

One of the independent or 'pirate' buses which competed with the largest operator, the General, in the mid-1920s. Buses were the most profitable part of London Transport, and the competition from 'pirates' was cause for concern for the Underground Group

From then on, the independent buses were gradually swallowed up until the coming of the Passenger Transport Board in 1933. But their activities and the relative profitability of buses in general, ensured that there was little investment money for new tube lines, even though the great increase in traffic around the capital made this a more and more pressing concern. One of the worst bottlenecks was at Finsbury Park Station. Here at rush hour, passengers trying to get to places not adequately served by the suburban steam railways had to leave the Piccadilly Line or the line from Moorgate and take a tram or a bus. The congestion at Finsbury Park became a great issue, but the Underground Group said there was no money to build new lines and, by an antiquated piece of legislation, the LNER mainline company could veto any extension into its 'territory' by the tube railways serving Finsbury Park. At a public inquiry into the situation in 1925, Press reports were read out which claimed that 'men and women fight like rugby footballers for means to reach their homes' and 'clothes are torn and fainting girls and women are so common as to pass almost without comment'.

Once again, it was government money which came to the rescue. In 1929, the newly-elected Labour administration offered funds for public utility works which would help reduce the growing number of unemployed. The Underground Group snapped up the opportunity and put forward its proposal to extend the Piccadilly Line from Finsbury Park to Wood Green, Arnos Grove, Southgate and Cockfosters. The expansionist policy was under way again, with thirty thousand free tickets offered to local residents travelling from Arnos Grove after 10.00 a.m. when that station was opened in 1932. And there was a new opportunity for Frank Pick to bring in his 'modernistic' architecture, with stations designed by Charles Holden.

Dipping into the same government unemployment relief kitty, the Metropolitan Railway found the money to improve its stations and rolling stock and to build a new line from Wembley Park to Stanmore, which was

Left: As the Piccadilly Line was extended to Cockfosters in the thirties, London Transport announced its coming with signs such as this. Oakwood was the name chosen for the new station. New tube lines were built with government funds provided for the relief of unemployment

Below: One of the show-piece stations designed by the architect Charles Holden on the Piccadilly Line extension. London Transport have retained the thirties' lighting in the interior of this station, which is now a listed building

completed in 1932. In fact, in the inter-war years, the bulk of the modernization and extension of London's tube system was financed by the Treasury.

The great achievement of these years was the co-ordination and modernization of a transport system which had been revolutionized by electric traction and motorization before 1914, but remained archaic in many ways. Travel on London Transport increased enormously, and the stations built in the days of Charles Tyson Yerkes could not cope. It was Frank Pick of the Underground Group who was the real genius of the modernization system, and it was his almost fanatical concern with providing London with the best transport system in the world that established the character of the buses and tubes which are now a sadly run-down relic of London Transport in its heyday.

Pick's attention to detail was legendary: he always wrote in green ink, so that his missives could be instantly recognized. Though not a very public figure, he personally investigated some aspect of the Underground Group (and later the Passenger Transport Board) activities every week. New Underground stations were designed not only to look pleasing and up-to-date: they were carefully planned to handle a very heavy traffic flow with maximum efficiency.

The escalators at Holborn Station in 1937. Londoners travelled around the capital much more in the inter-war years than they had ever done before, and one of the tasks of the operators was to redesign stations so that they could handle more traffic. The tasteful, reflected lighting of the period can still be seen at Southgate Station

THE NEW UNDERGROUND STATION AT PICCADILLY CIRCUS

Nearly four years were occupied in constructing this station, which is now capable of dealing with 50,000,000 passengers annually. Seven entrances are provided to the booking-hall, and these may be used also as a means of crossing the busy Circus in safety. Eleven escalators, each capable of being worked in either direction, as required, lead to the platforms, where 1,600 trains call daily.

The extraordinary labyrinth of the new Piccadilly Circus Station, opened in 1928. This was the most spectacular creation of the Underground Group: it attracted attention all over the world and a delegation was sent from Moscow to study it

Escalators, for example, replaced lifts in many central stations in the 1920s and 1930s. Pick's *pièce de résistance* was Piccadilly Circus Station, which had opened in 1906 as an old red-tiled Yerkes model but was hopelessly inadequate for the traffic of the 1920s. Whereas 1½ million passengers had used the station in 1907, the number had risen to 18 million by 1922. Pick chose the architect Charles Holden, designer of many new stations on the Piccadilly Line, for the major rebuilding project in the centre of town.

An entirely new labyrinth of tunnels was excavated below Eros in Piccadilly Circus, the statue being removed for safe-keeping for a couple of years while work proceeded. When the new station opened in 1928 it attracted world attention, with its Art Deco booking hall, subdued lighting, and shopping arcade. It was the new 'Heart of the Empire' and a specially commissioned painting adorned the interior, showing Piccadilly as the very centre of the world. This was Pick's vision of the Underground system – it was not simply a commercial enterprise, it expressed a Utopian vision.

The Underground Group was building itself a new headquarters at 55 Broadway, above St James's Park Station, at the same time as Piccadilly Circus was being redesigned. Again, the architect Charles Holden was brought in, and famous sculptors, including Henry Moore and Jacob Epstein were commissioned to provide works of art as part of the building's façade. They remain there today, as monuments to Pick's remarkable influence, largely unnoticed by passers-by who are aware only of the stark grey building towering above them.

Most of the redesign of London Transport was carried out before it finally became a public corporation in 1933. Its character was already established, and Lord Ashfield and Frank Pick, the two figures largely responsible for its creation before 1933, were put in control of the London Passenger Transport Board. Since the beginning of the century, the London County Council had been arguing that it was absurd for the capital's transport system to be left in the hands of a mass of competing private operators, and a number of inquiries and committees had recommended much greater co-ordination of services. But any kind of 'nationalization' was anathema.

The creation of a Passenger Transport Board became a possibility in 1929, when the first effective Labour Government was elected, and Herbert Morrison, the leading London Socialist politician of the day, became Transport Minister. He began work immediately to try to bring transport under public control. The fact that he was successful was due largely to Lord Ashfield's willingness to co-operate: Morrison, the Socialist politician, and Ashfield, the businessman concerned with rationalizing an industry which had never been very profitable, were by the early 1930s of similar mind. It was Ashfield who persuaded the Underground Group's shareholders that selling out to a public corporation was the way forward, and without his conviction that the system was best run in this way, public ownership would almost certainly have been delayed until the 1940s.

Exactly why Lord Ashfield was so keen to see the creation of the Passenger Transport Board, which excluded the mainline suburban services but brought in the Metropolitan Line and the LCC tram and trolley bus services, is unclear. But one of the main reasons must have been the recognition that running the transport system of a great metropolis was not immensely profitable. The Passenger Transport Board was still charged with covering its costs and presented exactly the same kind of managerial responsibilities and problems as running the Underground Group, but with the possibility of integrating all services and eliminating competition.

Ashfield and Pick pursued much the same policies as before when they took over the Transport Board, and still believed that in order to pay its way London's transport system had to expand, and in fact London itself would have to grow bigger. All the time people were moving out of the centre of London into the suburbs, and the tubes and buses had to follow. And in following, they in turn encouraged this outward movement.

More tube line extensions were planned: the Edgware Line would be continued to Bushey Heath. Work on laying out the line had begun when the Second World War put an end to this and other schemes. Though new lines were built in the 1940s, by 1939 the Underground system was almost complete, and the years of expansionist policy were over. London was now to be ringed by a 'Green Belt' to prevent further growth.

The public transport system itself was being threatened by the rapidly growing influence of the motor car. Lord Ashfield recognized this by the mid-1930s, and was issuing warnings to the Transport Board that the motorist was beginning to take traffic away from buses and Underground trains:

> The private car has completely revolutionized passenger transport. It has set higher standards of speed, convenience and even luxury, which must have their reactions on standards to be aimed at by those who provide public forms of passenger transport. Indeed, it may be said that failure to maintain a rising standard of comfort in our services, both rail and road, must have the effect of further increasing the competition of the private car.

And as early as 1933, Ashfield told Underground Group shareholders: 'The theatre traffic, which at one time was carried upon the railways and omnibuses, has now largely passed to the private car.'

By the 1930s, too, the motor car was beginning to worsen the traffic congestion in central London, already jammed with motor buses, taxis and goods vehicles. There were far fewer private cars than there are today – the great boom in car ownership did not take place until the 1950s – but the regulation of traffic in London as elsewhere was relatively primitive. Traffic lights were a rarity until the 1930s: the first set of electric signals in London – operated manually by policemen – were installed in Piccadilly Circus in 1925. White lines dividing lanes of traffic did not arrive until the 1930s, and constant road works and slow moving goods vehicles ensured that the traffic flow was generally slow in the centre of town.

However, the great pleasure of those who could afford cars in this period was to bomb out of town onto the country roads, or along the new by-passes that were being built. In 1930, speed limits were lifted completely, there were still no driving tests and the roads around London were used as a race track by Bright Young Things who bought cars built for speed. Lady Strickland can recall the madness of those early motoring days:

> My boyfriends, the very rich young men, they had marvellous cars, very fast cars, MGs, Bugattis, Bentleys. Of course, in those days you didn't have to pass a test, a friend took you out on the road a few times to learn the gears, then off you went. They did some terrible things. One friend of mine used to go up a very curvy road near Godalming on the wrong side for a thrill. He was killed quite quickly. Another one used to go over hump back bridges at seventy for a thrill, risking meeting something in the middle. My uncle tried to drive his MG over a passenger bridge in a railway station and was had up.
>
> After we'd been to three or four nightclubs in evening dress, we'd go down the Great West Road at about eighty, at three or four in the morning in the dark, to Cuckoo Weir near Windsor. I'd slip the dress off and the shoes and swim in all my heavy silver jewellery. And then it started to get

light and you had to clamber out with nothing on, it was great fun. My husband used to drive badly when he'd had a bit to drink and I remember threatening to swallow the ignition keys unless he let me drive.

As the motor car replaced horse-drawn vehicles, the number of accidents on the roads rose rapidly. In 1901, just before the first cars began to replace the horse-drawn carriages of the aristocracy, there were 186 fatal road accidents in the London County Council area. By 1929, when the wealthy all had cars and the capital's roads were full of motor buses and lorries, fatalities reached 1,362 and there were 55,000 injuries. The slaughter was such that in 1934 a new law brought in the 30 miles per hour speed limit and driving tests.

But as motorists began to be more effectively controlled, so their numbers rose rapidly. By 1939 there were two million cars in Britain, a quarter of them registered in London and the Home Counties. As mass production stepped up, so the price of cars fell. The first £100 British car was the Morris Minor Tourer of 1931, but it was relatively primitive in engineering terms and did not sell widely. The real breakthrough came in 1935 when Ford produced the 'Popular' for £100. Many other models were offered by manufacturers for just over £100, and hire purchase terms became easier.

At the Earls Court Motor Show of 1939, Austin, for example, offered the Austin Seven at £108 to £129; the Austin 'Big' Seven at £137 to £149. 10s; the Austin Ten at £175 to £189; and a range which included four more models with prices reaching £700 or more. By this time, many suburban semi-detached

A vintage pile-up on the Finchley Road in 1924. The arrival of the motor car in London greatly increased road accidents, which reached a peak in the 1930s before driving tests were brought in

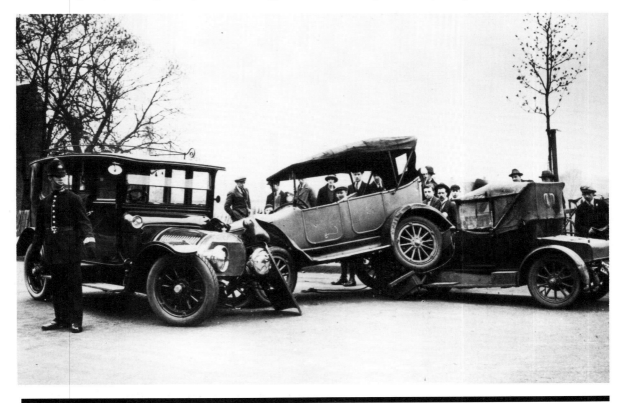

houses were being built with garages attached, though the potential market was over-estimated as a large proportion remained empty of motor cars until the 1950s. Mass ownership had not really quite begun when the Second World War broke out.

However, transport planners and politicians were aware of the threat posed by the car. In 1936, a report on traffic congestion in central London was prepared by Sir Charles Bressey, a former chief engineer of the Ministry of Transport, and Sir Edwin Lutyens, one of the most famous architects of the day. They listed all the trouble spots in London, sent vehicles through the centre on test runs, timed hold-ups, estimated the costs in lost hours, and proposed new roads which would have carved right through the middle of the capital.

This period really marked the beginning of the end of London's public transport heyday, for the motor car was soon to cream off a whole lot of 'leisure travel' as Lord Ashfield had feared. Already in the 1930s, new tube stations on the extensions to the Piccadilly Line incorporated car parks, whereas stations of the 1920s had made provision only for buses.

London Transport had expanded so rapidly between the wars, and had become such a powerful vehicle for the empire building of Ashfield and Pick because at precisely the time when the need and ability of Londoners to travel more frequently and over longer distances had greatly increased, *public* transport was for the majority the only available means. In America, where mass car ownership arrived much earlier, public transport – particularly the well-organized Inter-Urban rail service – was undermined much sooner. In London, however, public transport retained its dominant position until 1939, by which time London Transport could boast with some justification that it was the best-run system in the world.

Motoring down the Kingston By-pass in 1938. Though cars were causing problems in the centre of London, this was the heyday of the open road out of town

CHAPTER FOUR

THE BATTLE FOR THE SUBURBS

DAVIS ESTATES L^{TD}

BUILDERS OF HOMES

YOUR GUARANTEE
DAVIS BUILT

TRAVEL OUT of London by car or train in any direction, and after about eight to ten miles' journey from the centre you reach a border land where the scenery changes suddenly and completely. It's almost like a geological break in the structure of the rock, with one historical flow of bricks and mortar being deposited and ceasing to expand, while another, later, flow begins. You are leaving the built-up limits of Victorian and Edwardian London, and entering the vast expanse of a very different and much newer London. The sky-line is lower, the doors and windows of the houses are smaller, and everything from the tube station to the shopping precinct is built on a reduced scale, so that it has an oddly toy-like quality. You are in semi-detached suburbia.

The very term 'semi-detached' is evocative of a kind of tidy, private, polished, vacuumed way of life, in which the horizon extends no further than the garden shed. It seems to be a denial of the great metropolis which it surrounds like a gnome-built reef, and intellectuals and architects have generally dismissed the whole thing as a kind of cultural disaster, without vision or style. In his cuttingly comical classification of building design, *A Cartoon History of Architecture*, Osbert Lancaster dubbed much of it 'By-pass Variegated', a catch-all term for the jumble of mock-Tudor and faintly modernist influences in design. Nobody thinks of suburbia as exciting, except in the sense that it induces in those who hate it a fierce indignation.

But the story of how it was built, and how during an era which is largely remembered for its Depression and disappointment, this new suburbia arose at such a rate that it doubled the size of the capital in twenty years, is every bit as intriguing as any episode in London's history. And though the new London that was created may not appear in itself to be an exciting place, the forces which gave rise to it and the political battles involved were as fierce as any that took place in the previous century.

For the nature and appearance of semi-detached London reflects an historical revolution in social life and social policy which began before the First World War, was influenced by the experience of the war itself, and took shape in the troubled years of peace, when fears of a Communist revolution were real, and the propagandist catch-phrase, 'Homes fit for Heroes', had not yet been dismissed as a politician's pipe-dream.

There was, in a sense, a battle for the new suburbs between two political ideals; the first, of public provision for the mass of the population; and the second, of allowing private builders and landowners to provide Londoners with homes. And though there was some doubt in the early 1920s which would be dominant, there was no question that private housing was the victor by the end of the period. Of the enormous number of new houses built around London between the wars – something like 700,000 – three-quarters were put up by private builders for home-owners. Though the London County Council began in a confident mood in the twenties to create its own kind of

Previous pages, left: A Davis Estates brochure for 'sun-trap' semi-detached houses, a characteristic design of the late thirties. A private building boom between the wars pushed back London's suburban frontiers, doubling the size of the capital

Right: Roehampton, a London County Council 'cottage' estate of the 1920s. There was in a sense a battle of the suburbs over what sort of housing – council or private – should be built, and where, during the inter-war years

municipal suburbia with funds provided by the government, by the 1930s it had run into a host of social and economic difficulties which forced it to pull back and to put its greatest effort into slum clearance in the centre of the capital. The battle for the suburbs was won decisively by the building society, the landowners and the home-owner.

However, in terms of style and philosophy, both council and private estate building of the period was influenced by the same reforming ideas which had arisen at the end of the nineteenth century in response to the unplanned and often squalid nature of the Victorian city. In the eighteenth century, the larger and wealthier landowners in London had attempted, often with some success, to impose a kind of planning on their estates, forbidding the entry of noxious trades into their new streets and squares and often defending their developments with gates and gatekeepers. But the pressure of London's relatively impoverished majority, as well as the loosening of estate control, combined in the nineteenth century to undermine such planning, and the ideal of *laissez-faire* discouraged any kind of state control in town planning.

The idea that on the fringes of town a pleasant, semi-rural environment could be created for Londoners, away from the smoke and noise of industry, first emerged in the late nineteenth century. An innovative development was built at Bedford Park, Chiswick, as early as 1878. Here you can see the beginnings of what was to evolve into the semi-detached house. But it was in 1898 that the concept was crystallized by Ebenezer Howard in his book *Garden Cities of Tomorrow*, in which he analysed the advantages and disadvantages of town and country. The first provided excitement, entertainment and jobs; the second offered natural beauty, a healthy environment and cheaper housing. The town was polluted and overcrowded; the country did not provide jobs or entertainment. Howard's garden city would offer the best of both worlds in a planned environment which kept home and work apart, but not too far so that the misery of daily commuting would be minimized.

What Howard proposed was not suburban development but quite new towns around London. These would have a population limited to about 30,000 people of all social classes, and would be surrounded by a 'Green Belt' separating them from the built-up area of London. He would have liked government backing to carry out his dream of building such places, but before 1914 the state did not provide funds for putting up houses or towns. So Howard got private backing for his ventures at Letchworth, begun in 1903, and Welwyn Garden City, where building started in 1920.

Howard's vision was immediately appealing and, in a diluted form, influenced other pre-war developments, such as the privately-built Hampstead Garden Suburb, begun as the new Hampstead Underground Line was being extended into the fields of Golders Green in 1907. It also influenced a mock-Tudor revival in the early years of the twentieth century that expressed a nostalgia for a lost world of rustic innocence and sturdy country folk. In the public sphere, too, Howard's ideals were also having some effect. For example, the London County Council in the early 1900s began a policy of building new garden suburb-style estates on the edges of London at Norbury and White Hart Lane, Tottenham.

These were the prototypes of the two styles which would flourish in the inter-war years and dominate London's ever-expanding suburban landscape. On the one hand there would be largely unplanned speculator suburbs for those who could afford a semi-rural retreat, fresh air and the modern conveniences of a new home. And on the other there would be 'cottage' style estates – often carefully planned and architect-designed but much more modest in their architecture and amenities – provided for the working classes to rent by the LCC and local councils.

But the First World War put an end to building altogether. It was this hiatus which ultimately was to ensure that Victorian and inter-war styles of building were to look so very different from each other, for London did not begin to grow again until the 1920s, when the world had changed. As nothing had been done during the war to improve the conditions of the poor, and hardly any housing of any kind had been constructed, there was a serious shortage of homes in 1918. During the four years of the war rent strikes by militant munitions workers had managed to win a freeze on rents in poorer housing, and at the lower end of the market had taken away any incentive landlords may have had – which was not much – to provide rented accommodation for working people. Shortly after the war, this rent freeze was extended to higher income groups, in recognition of the fact that there was a desperate shortage of private, rented accommodation for the middle classes and that without such a constraint, landlords could have charged what they liked.

Prices had risen steeply, and there was a shortage of raw materials as well as labour, which made house-building costly and difficult. There was little incentive, moreover, for people to invest in housing for rent. Before 1914 it was quite common for small investors to take out a mortgage on a house which was then rented to someone else. The mortgage paid a fixed rate of interest over an indefinite period and could be sold at any time. After the war, not only rents, but the interest paid on such mortgages, was frozen. Investing in property was no longer 'safe as houses' as the saying had been before 1914.

It appeared unlikely, therefore, that private developers would be able to build the 'Homes fit for Heroes' that were promised in return for the sacrifices of the war. This presented the government with a serious problem for, unless something was done to improve housing conditions, there seemed a real prospect of serious social unrest or even a revolution. For the First World War had involved the effort of the whole nation – including women who took over armaments work, helped to run the transport system and kept industry going – and people had been led to expect something in return. The situation was made even more worrying for the government because it felt it could no longer depend on the traditional loyalty of the army to quell any major disturbances. After 1916, when conscription was introduced, it was no longer a professional band, but a mass of ordinary men, still armed until they were demobilized, and therefore potentially dangerous. Fears were heightened by a wave of mutinies and soldiers' strikes in 1919, by men frustrated with the slowness of their return to civilian life.

In addition, race riots against immigrant groups who settled in ports like London after the war, youth riots against the police on the capital's streets, and a police strike for better pay and conditions all seemed to point to an

impending breakdown of law and order immediately after the war. And, of course, this was an era of revolutions in Europe – of which the most disturbing for the British ruling class was the Russian Revolution of 1917 – and politicians like Lloyd George were frightened that shattered dreams of a better life might trigger a similar Socialist revolution at home.

It was against this background that for the first time in history a British government decided to put national funds into house building. In 1919, what became known as the Addison Act – after the Minister of Health who initiated it – was passed giving generous grants to local authorities to put up new housing; any cost above a one penny rate was borne by the government. In effect, this was a *carte blanche* for councils to build as many houses as they wanted, and a great many took up the offer with enthusiasm. Among them was the single largest housing authority in the capital, the London County Council, which not only began to extend its existing pre-war estates on the fringes of London, but went out to buy new land to plan new estates. A special study commissioned in 1918 from the Liberal M.P. Sir Tudor Walters had recommended a very high standard of house construction, with a bathroom for each unit, and a low density of building limited to twelve houses to the acre. Armed with all the money they needed, and some of the ideals of the garden city movement, as well as instructions to produce high-quality dwellings, the LCC set to work.

In 1920, an estate was begun in Roehampton in south-west London, on the site of what had been a private park owned by an American financier. In the same year, building began at Bellingham near Catford in south London, and at Becontree in Essex, on open land way out to the east of London. Of these, Becontree was to become by far the largest – in fact the single biggest council development in the world.

Montrose Avenue, Watling, in the course of construction in 1926, with a special railway, where the road would later run, for ferrying in building materials. Twenties' council estates like this were the 'Homes fit for Heroes' promised by the government in return for the sacrifices of the Great War

Other London councils took advantage of the generous Addison Act, and between 1919 and 1922, something approaching 30,000 local authority houses were built in Greater London. This represented sixty per cent of all housing put up in the period, as compared with only six per cent built by councils before 1914. The quality, as well as quantity, of council house-building in this period was high. As the average houses had three or four bedrooms, an inside toilet and bathroom, hot and cold running water, and front and back gardens, they must have seemed idyllic for those leaving the run-down rented accommodation of inner London. The 624 houses completed at Roehampton under the Addison Act are good examples of the standard of building achieved in this short-lived period, when the 'Homes fit for Heroes' dream appeared to be coming true.

But in 1921, the dream ended as abruptly as it had begun. An economic crisis led to cuts in public spending, and the generous subsidies for council housing that had alarmed the Treasury were withdrawn. Councils, which had been spending at a tremendous rate during the two-year bonanza of the Addison Act, some buying properties built by private builders for £1000 and renting them to tenants, had to cut back. Never again in the inter-war period did they provide the generous kind of accommodation of the early Roehampton houses, though subsidies were renewed, and then withdrawn, as the political climate changed in the twenties and thirties. And all the time there was a belief among Conservatives that private builders could solve the housing problem. From 1919, subsidies were offered to builders putting up cheap semi-ds for rent or sale, and in 1923 this aid to the home owner was increased as grants became more generous and the government made it

Bricklayers and carpenters working on the massive Becontree estate in 1924. The inter-war housing boom was boosted by a large pool of cheap labour working long hours for low wages

easier for people to get mortgages on lower-priced housing by allowing councils to offer them or to guarantee payments to building societies. In a period when private building was still in the doldrums this was important for its survival, and represented a critical shift of finance and encouragement away from council housing and towards the private home owner.

Nevertheless the 'cottage' estates which the LCC had begun on the fringes of London continued to expand under new laws which varied in their generosity and effects. It took eighteen years to complete the vast Becontree Estate, with a railway line built through it to carry building materials up from the Thames, and fifty miles of roads laid out as it pushed north and eastwards into Essex. By the time it was finished, Becontree had a population of nearly 120,000 and was already bigger than many English provincial towns – Bath for example. Though the uniformity of housing of the estate was often a cause for criticism, the ever-changing laws on subsidies ensured considerable variation in style; generally speaking, as time went on houses became smaller and less convenient. Minor conveniences, like a handbasin in the bathroom and plaster in the scullery, which were standard fittings in Roehampton houses, were no longer provided.

However, throughout the 1920s, the LCC continued to pursue a policy of buying land on the outskirts of the capital, beyond its own boundaries, to establish new cottage estates. It was able to do so because the Wheatley Act, passed by the Labour Government in 1924, gave relatively generous subsidies for council house building. The LCC began to build estates at Watling in north London, on the route of the tube line extension to Edgware, at White City in west London, and to the south near Morden, on an estate named St Helier after a former LCC councillor. These estates continued to expand until the early 1930s, but by that time the council-building boom on the

A bumper harvest in Gaskarth Road, Watling, in 1929. With their gardens, inside toilets and bathrooms, these council homes seemed like dreamland to many of those moving out from run-down inner London

fringes of London was well and truly over. State-funded suburbia had run into many difficulties – for example, living out in the suburbs and paying higher rents and travelling costs proved prohibitively expensive for many working-class people. But, most important, council housing was unable to compete with private housing, into which the nation's small investors poured their money.

The peak year for local authority building had been 1927, but it had already been overtaken by private building, which by chance had benefited from the very same economic and political twists and turns which first put money into council housing, then took it out again. For the building of London's private, semi-detached suburbia was not simply the result of the rise of an ideal of a quasi-rural existence amongst the moderately well-off middle classes: it was made possible and encouraged by an economic revolution, in which a large part of the nation's investments were poured into housing.

Before 1914, only a very small proportion of English people owned their own home. People rented their housing, whatever their social class, and many people put their savings into property for a small but steady return. After the Great War, as we have seen, that system collapsed as far as new building was concerned because of the freeze on rents and on the interest from mortgages, and because of the high cost of building. However, since the eighteenth century a building society movement had been developing in Britain, its origins tracing back to friendly societies and freehold societies. These were relatively small groups of people who got together to acquire property and build houses for one reason or another. The freehold societies, for instance, had originally been set up as a means to win the vote, which was only enjoyed by the owners of plots of land worth 40s. Many of these societies were wound up after a few years, but others remained in existence after the founders had acquired their property, and so called themselves *permanent* building societies. Though these societies had been established originally to encourage or enable relatively small groups of artisans and middle-class people to become property owners, they began to attract investors who wanted a safe place to salt away their money.

But the virtual disappearance of house-building for rent after 1918 and the loss of all kinds of overseas investment brought about by the war, greatly increased the incentive to invest in building societies. They were helped by considerable government sympathy for home ownership. During the war, taxes had risen from 1s to 5s in the pound, and the building societies were able to negotiate a private deal with the Inland Revenue whereby their investors paid these higher taxes at source, which worked out at a rate lower than that paid on income from other investments. It saved the taxman collection costs and made building society investments much more attractive.

An even better deal for investors was negotiated in 1921, and the funds of small investors began to flow steadily into building societies. Immediately after the war, the largest building societies had been located in the North of England, but a series of amalgamations, as well as the steady take-off of house-building in the South, changed the situation so that half of the biggest societies were in the South by the 1930s.

Throughout the 1920s, the amount of money available for private house-building for sale therefore increased steadily, and the number of people to whom home-ownership appealed grew at the same time. This was for a number of related reasons. First, the number of white-collar workers, clerks and lower-grade professionals multiplied, creating in effect a middle class that was much larger, but rather poorer on average, than its Victorian counterpart. For this emerging social group, domestic servants were a luxury. The young girl who might have become a maid-of-all-work and cook found that there were many rival jobs in industry, catering and hotels which pushed up her wages. Whereas the wealthier families of the West End were able to hang on to a living-in staff of maids and cooks, the middle class in general rapidly gave up the employment of servants. At the same time, the age of marriage fell steadily, so that the number of new households – that is, husband and wife wanting to set up a separate home from their parents – rose, while the number of children in the average family fell. The result was that there were more, but smaller, households, in search of smaller, more convenient, housing.

Buying a home, and investing in a building society, are two sides of the same coin, and the attraction of exchanging rented accommodation for a 'home of one's own' was increased by the feeling of financial uncertainty that many middle-class people experienced in the inter-war years. So by the mid-1920s, the supply of money for home ownership, as well as the demand, were created by much the same social and economic forces. The first slump, in 1921, followed by the Depression of 1929-31, greatly increased the attractions of investment in building societies, as the future of manufacturing industry seemed to be so uncertain.

So the idea of home ownership caught on, and the building of private suburban houses increased steadily after 1922, rapidly outstripping the output of local authorities. Land was relatively cheap on the outskirts of London because agriculture was depressed, and the large landowners one by one began to sell plots to builders. And just as the building societies grew in size, so did a number of building firms, many of whom moved from the North of England to cash in on the London market. Taylor Woodrow, Costain, Laing and Wimpey were among those who expanded in the inter-war years during the house-building bonanza.

From about 1926 onwards, as the new machinery for building private suburbia for home-ownership was gathering momentum, the LCC's attempts to create idyllic, semi-rural 'home and hearth' settlements on the fringes of London were running into trouble. The LCC planners and architects were proud of their achievements, and in their way had taken considerable care in house design, within the constraints imposed by the ups and downs of government financial support. But the planners' vision had not been matched on the ground, for the people who went to live in the new estates were confronted with many difficulties, even though the houses they lived in were far superior to anything they had known before.

In fact it was not the poorest of Londoners who were allowed to move to the 'out-county' estates in the first place. A whole constellation of factors combined to prevent the poor from escaping from the inner-city slums. Those applying for new accommodation were required to provide a regular and

Hatfield Street, part of a pocket of slumland poverty near Waterloo Station in 1923. Most poor people like this could not afford to move out to the new council estates

punctual record of rent payments, and the visiting LCC inspector would check the rent book to determine this. He would also note whether or not the family was of clean and respectable appearance – this was widely accepted as the litmus test of good character, which in turn was likely to influence whether or not a family would be good tenants on the cottage estates. The LCC understandably wanted to recruit respectable tenants who could be relied on to give the lie to the middle-class fear that their suburbs were being invaded by hordes of roughs. But poor families, almost by definition, frequently got into rent arrears during seasonal slumps and hard times, and it was a constant and sometimes unsuccessful struggle to keep large families and overcrowded rooms looking respectable when it all had to be done on a shoestring budget. Many poor families, then, fell at the first hurdle.

But many more families were to be excluded by the ruling – rigorously imposed in the early 1920s – that their income had to be five times greater than what they would spend each week on rent, rates and fares to work. The rents themselves were quite high – on average 11s to 15s a week in the 1920s. So were transport costs, which could frequently mount up to 10s a week since most estates were essentially 'out-county' dormitories, situated several miles away from where most breadwinners actually worked. This was particularly marked in Becontree, which had only one station located in the first part of the estate to be built; this left the rest for years without adequate transport into London, where nearly everyone worked. As the majority of unskilled and semi-skilled workers in central London earned only about £3 a week at this time, large numbers had simply no chance of qualifying for a council cottage.

Also in the first years there were few or no schools on the new estates, partly because of the opposition of local education authorities to LCC cottage estate schemes – they were not keen to spend money educating exported Londoners and were often sluggish in their provision – so hundreds of children spent months or years roaming the streets when they should have been at school. Thus the suburban council tenant was stranded in a vast and often inhospitable environment without the economic means, available more generally to home-owners, to do anything about it. And there was no single authority within the Greater London area which could co-ordinate transport, education, health and housing in such a way that the 'garden city' ideal was even approached. As a result there was a massive turnover of tenants on the early estates, sometimes as high as twenty per cent a year.

At the same time, opposition to LCC 'out-county' estates was often fierce. Local authorities outside the county area did not want poor people billeted on them, as this lowered the tone of their area, threatened to increase the rate burden and might discourage better-off people from moving in. In 1924, for example, the LCC tried to buy some land in Edgware and, despite the fact that it was not the poorest of Londoners who would ever be offered homes in such a district, the *Golders Green Gazette* was quick to respond: ' . . . this will lead to a big slum development; impairing the good work already in hand in the north of the Chandos estate, and completely "knocking out" any chance of private residential development at Burnt Oak.'

Often local authorities in these outlying districts were prepared to house what they thought of as their 'own' working classes in their council houses, but they did not want the LCC's poor. Thus when the LCC began to expand the Downham Estate, near Bromley, local residents objected at an enquiry saying: 'Such a scheme will reduce the respectability of the . . . streets by inundating the neighbourhood with working classes.'

In fact, in 1926 the sensitive residents of a private estate which abutted the southern edge of Downham took the law into their own hands and actually built a brick wall across a road that led straight from the private part of the street to the council houses. Bromley Council refused to co-operate with LCC demands for its demolition, and it was not pulled down until the early years of the Second World War when it impeded emergency services. The inconvenience and bad feeling caused by this 'Berlin Wall' are still vivid in the memories of local people, like Betty Trigg:

It was about seven feet high and it had broken glass on the top. Well, when I was a child I lived in the council houses and we used to climb over the wall because we used to scrump apples and throw things up at the conker trees to get the conkers down – there were trees over on the Bromley side, you see. And of course they didn't like us doing that, we got shouted at. As I grew older I realized how inconvenient the wall was for the mothers, because to catch the bus to Bromley they had to do a detour with the wall being there.

I used to live in the house next to the wall on the council side. One day a young girl decided it wasn't right to have a wall up there when there was a war imminent, and she decided she'd start knocking a lump off it. I suppose there were about a dozen teenagers around her, encouraging her, but the police came and stopped her.

The story of the Downham Wall is a small but graphic illustration of the kind of opposition the LCC and its tenants faced in territory regarded not only by private residents and local authorities, but by many Conservative politicians as well, as the preserve of the middle classes. In fact the LCC, dominated

The Downham Wall, built across the middle of a road leading from a council to a private estate – this view is from the private side. The aim of this 'Berlin Wall' was to prevent council tenants and their children from infiltrating into a quiet, respectable middle-class neighbourhood. The wall illustrates the opposition the LCC faced when trying to house working-class people in the suburbs

politically by the Conservative Municipal Reform Party until 1934, had incorporated this notion in its original plans for cottage estates: one of the four basic principles it adopted was to take into account the possible detrimental effects on middle-class areas of large-scale working-class developments.

Another principle, however, simply encouraged the fears of those who wanted to keep the LCC out. This was that it should build on a large scale so as to economize on costs, and at the same time create a new and distinctive social life for the residents. Becontree was so vast that its example terrified any district that thought the LCC might be moving in. And because large-scale low-density housing used up so much land – despite the fact that the LCC never put up as many houses as it intended – the search for available sites was already becoming a problem in the late 1920s.

This problem was aggravated by the restrictions on land use commonly imposed by the aristocratic families who owned some of the land on which the new suburbs were built. Some landed families – following an essentially nineteenth-century practice of trying to ensure that any land they leased would be used for up-market housing – would only sell part or the whole of their estate on the condition that it was used for superior, low density housing developments. Thus when Blendon Hall, an old-established country seat standing in 88 acres of parkland near Bexley in Kent, was put on the market in 1928 following the death of the owner, the widow, faced with heavy death duties and wishing to move away from the district, made a series of stipulations – backed by the urban district council – when she sold it to developers. Amongst these stipulations on what became the Blendon Estate, were the preservation of the Hall, its immediate grounds and the most beautiful parts of the estate, no building to be erected within fifty feet of a main road, and a maximum housing density of eight to the acre. Large landowners were anxious not to spoil the beauty of their old estate with a mass of council cottages or cheap rows of private houses. And they stood to lose financially by cheap development because they usually sold their estates piecemeal and wanted to retain the value of the remaining land. In this way, they established in the 1920s a reputation for opposition to down-market building on or near their grounds.

Partly as a result of these sorts of difficulties, by the late 1920s the LCC planners seem to have had a change of heart, and they began to think again in terms of rehousing the poor in the centre of town, not in 'cottages' but in grand blocks of flats. This in many ways provided the fashionable architect of the day with a more interesting challenge. But here the LCC still experienced difficulties in finding the sites on which to build: land assembly in the centre of town was not easy. So when, in 1929, a Labour Government came to power at Westminster, launched a slum-clearance drive, and put money back into the system, the LCC valuers set out again on a land hunt on the suburban fringes of the capital. But they were far too late.

The slump of 1929-31 gave building societies a tremendous boost, as they became the easiest, safest and most profitable place for investors to put their money. The story of the Abbey Road Building Society provides a colourful example. It was formed in 1874, and takes its name from its first address, Abbey Road, NW6. The founders were members of the Free Church and met in a schoolroom attached to the chapel. By the outbreak of war in 1914 the Society had assets of £750,000.

Above: Clerks at the Abbey Road Building Society wade through the torrent of paperwork created by the massive growth in home ownership. The Abbey's assets grew from £¾ million in 1914 to over £46 million in 1935

Left: A 1930s-style National Building Society brochure – the National later amalgamated with the Abbey to become the Abbey National. This sort of propaganda, which helped to fuel the building society boom, stressed the good sense and security of home ownership, and dismissed renting – which until the 1920s was the norm – as throwing money down the drain

By 1925, assets had increased to £3.5 million, and it was developing rapidly into a modern-style building society, drawing funds from a wide range of investors and advertising itself extensively to both investors and borrowers. It had grown to such a size by 1927 that it moved out of Abbey Road and built a new headquarters in Upper Baker Street. Between 1929 and 1935 its assets rose dramatically from £19.1 million to £46.1 million, and outgrowing yet again its headquarters it moved in 1932 to another head office in the street, the clock-tower of which is still a landmark today. It amalgamated with the National, to become Abbey National, in 1944.

The Woolwich had been founded earlier, in 1847, and was a substantial local society by the turn of the century, its strength founded on the contributions of working men from Woolwich Arsenal. It too 'took off' after the First World War, its assets rising from £1.6 million to £27.1 million by 1934. It began to open branches all over London, in the City, in Ilford and Romford in Essex, in Finsbury Park, Ealing and many other of the expanding semi-detached suburbs.

So no problems were encountered with the funds for private building, and the building societies were soon in league with large building firms to make it easier for people to buy their own homes. A system of builders' 'pools' was agreed whereby the developer of an estate would underwrite the initial cost of acquiring houses so that the first-time buyer – as most people were – had to put down only five per cent, instead of twenty per cent of the cost. At the same time building society propaganda stressed the stupidity of paying rent.

One builder, Laing, estimated that the pooling system tripled the rate of house sales, and by the 1930s the whole private housing system was thriving. Whenever a new electric railway station opened, as on the Edgware or Morden Lines in the 1920s, semi-detached suburbia would develop at an astonishing rate. In south London, it was not uncommon for a developing builder to put up the money to make a contribution to the building of a railway station which would open up land for building. Houses were built along the new arterial roads in north, west and east London, along by-passes – anywhere that promised some access to the centre of town and local shopping precincts that sprung up at some focal point in the unplanned developments. For example, soon after the opening of the Kingston By-pass in 1927, it became lined with rows of spec'-built houses, as well as shops, pubs and factories. This came to be known as the problem of ribbon development, which was a public nuisance for many reasons, not least because it blocked through-roads with local traffic and pedestrians. Eventually – but too late to prevent most of London's arterial roads being sandwiched in by spec'-built housing – this nightmare of unplanned development was controlled by special legislation, the Ribbon Development Act of 1935, which gave local councils the power to restrict frontage developments along main roads.

A further boost to this building boom was given by the fall in price of raw materials during and after the slump, and by a lowering of the wages of building workers who – despite all this activity – were in constant supply as industry outside London declined. This pool of unemployed or under-employed labourers enabled employers to demand a long working week of forty-seven hours, and to keep wage rates down to a meagre 1s 8d an hour.

Above: A grand arched entrance to the Wates' Heathway Park Estate at Mitcham. Because it was a buyer's market, builders in the thirties launched brash advertising campaigns offering free furniture, fridges, season tickets, and the like, to sell their houses

When a job came to an end, or when depression hit the building industry in the winter months due to bad weather, some of these men who helped to build the new London suburbs – navvies, brickies, painters and plasterers – found themselves on the bread line. John Neary was one of the many Irish labourers who can remember what it was like to work on London's building sites in the days when you could be hired and fired on a daily or weekly basis:

Below: New Ideal Homestead's brochures in the 1930s. House prices have never been so low as they were at this time – a £5 deposit secured a cheap home in the leafy suburbs

> You'd tramp from one building site to another, and when you got there you'd sleep rough out in the fields sometimes – that would impress the foreman that you were tough and he'd be more likely to give you work. I used to dig manholes and trenches, and it was tough digging manholes. It would be six foot square and each man was given a manhole to dig and very often the last man to dig his manhole was fired. And when you were digging a trench, if you were working alongside one of the navvies, great big hefty men that could down twenty pints a day, they might try and 'dig you out',

dig much more than you, and if they did that and showed you up, you might have to go as well.

It was a very hard life, in the mornings, about one minute to eight, the foreman would come out and let out a big shout, particularly the Irish foremen – they were demons. He'd shout, 'jump to it, you so and so's', and people never answered back, and very often he would go along the trench and look down and he'd shout, 'if I don't see steam rising off your bloody backs I'll know you're not working'. And we'd always be stripped to the waist, whatever time of year it was, because they said it was a bad sign if a man worked with his jacket on, he wasn't sweating.

All sorts of people moved into the building business, and estate agents' clerks frequently set up on their own in an effort to make a fortune in the boom. Scouts scoured the countryside in search of new sites. And house prices fell as a result of fierce competition between builders and an eventual over-supply. House prices have never been so low as they were in the early 1930s, falling to £395 or occasionally less, with an average figure of about £500.

Builders began a massive campaign to sell estates, and houses came to be sold in almost the same way as other mass-produced consumer goods that were coming on the market. New developments were advertised with fire-work displays, concerts, visits from politicians and in one case, in Surbiton, a free car in the garage for the purchaser of a diminutive detached house. Film and radio stars were brought in to give a glamourous launch to very ordinary estates, and a whole range of newspaper advertising in the mass circulation dailies were used to lure the middle classes into the suburbs. Among the free gifts on offer to purchasers were railway season tickets, fridges and furniture. Modern Homes Ltd actually tried to entice buyers to its relatively expensive estate at Joel Park in Pinner, where houses were on sale from £850 to £1500, with an electric refrigerator, washing machine, cooker and seven fires free in each home.

This building bonanza spawned a great variety of private estates. The 'up-market' ones, comprising substantial semi-detached and detached residences, were concentrated for the most part in London's northern and north-western suburbs; for example in Edgware, Southgate and Northwood. Characteristically these would be cottage-style houses made up of a mish-mash of period decorative features, the most popular of which were mock Tudor. Timbered gables, elaborate porches with red tiled roofs, lattice and coloured glass windows, oak doors with Gothic panels, plus the inevitable bay windows, were all highly fashionable and helped to evoke a rural-romantic image. The period styling continued indoors with oak-panelled halls and dining rooms.

The keynote of the private inter-war estates was individuality and spec' builders with a keen eye for the middle-class market made architectural variety a major selling point, and ensured that every home could boast some unique decorative detail, however insignificant. Many homes would be given their own names, such as 'Dunroamin', 'Coze-cot', 'The Gables', and so on, for this was the land of the 1930s-style successful Mr Pooter, whose house was not only the sentimental centrepiece of his life, but also a supreme statement of his family's social status. The whole enterprise has been much criticized – both at the time and since – for its banality, pretentiousness and ugliness, but there is little doubt that the builders gave the home owners what they wanted, which was an 'olde worlde' style retreat, and definitely not the clean lines and concrete and glass of the modern movement.

There was also a hugh potential demand for more 'down-market' properties. With firms such as New Ideal Homesteads making available homes in places like Sidcup for a £5 deposit and as little as 8s 1d a week repayment, home ownership became a real possibility for many lower middle-class families and also for a substantial minority of working-class people – the proportion of working-class home owners rose from around five per cent in 1929 to fourteen per cent in 1939. They would live in much smaller semi-d's or in short terraced rows, with appropriately scaled down architectural details and sometimes just one reception room and two bedrooms. Even clerks, whose salaries and security nosedived with the financial crashes of the period, could just about scrape together enough for the deposit and mortgage repayment on a cheap home in the new suburbs – as Dora Dyer recalls:

> My husband was chief teller in a private American bank, and when the Wall Street Crash happened he lost his job. From then on he was a tally clerk in the docks and we had very little money coming in. Anyway, I couldn't stand it, living in our rooms any more, it was driving me mad, we lived just off the Old Kent Road and it was rough around there. I knew they were building a lot of houses down Sidcup way, so I went down one day. I saw a house I liked – it was £250 but it was yours for £5 down – then I came back that evening and told my husband we were moving. He said, 'alright you can move but you'll move on your own, you know we've got no prospects at the moment'. Anyway, he eventually agreed, and I had a friend with an open top lorry. We tied what little furniture we had on with ropes, and when we pulled up outside our new home you should have seen the look on our neighbours' faces, they were horrified, thought we were rough. I only had one room downstairs and one bedroom furnished, all the rest was floorboards, but we managed.

But even the very low mortgage repayments on the cheapest of houses were often too much for those earning the average wage of £3 10s a week. Fares, rates and other expenses, in addition to the mortgage repayment, might amount to nearly half of that sum. Even at rock bottom prices, the suburbs remained therefore the home of better-off Londoners – with one romantic, and little-known, exception. There were, after the Great War, some Londoners who had neither the means to buy a suburban house, nor the qualification or inclination to become council tenants. Yet they had been gripped by the suburban impulse which swept the capital, and longed, like so many after the war, for a 'home and heart' in some peaceful rural setting.

These were the 'plotlanders', suburban frontiersmen and women who set out to build their dream home in the country with their own hands. They might live in London during the week, in miserable privately rented accommodation, but at weekends they could set out for the countryside, usually beyond even the most far-flung of the railway suburbs and council estates, to a plot of their own. Farmers in Essex, in particular, were only too keen to sell off poor parts of their farms during the agricultural depression and these patches of pasture could be bought for a few pounds. To begin with, that was all that was there, until the plotlander pitched a tent and, bit by bit, began to build.

To places like Pitsea, Peacehaven, Laindon and Canvey Island they carted out bits of timber, often carrying building materials on bicycles, and created shanty towns which caused much greater shocks to the idealistic planners of the day than the sprouting suburbs proper. Anything with a roof might serve as a holiday and weekend home: disused railway carriages, garden sheds, ex-army huts and bus bodies. In time, a more elegant edifice might take shape and the family might settle there. Some of these shanty towns became quite large, attracting a rather unusual social mix of bohemians, back-to-the-landers, and working-class families with the home-owner's pride but without the resources for a 'proper home'.

These shanty towns are still fondly remembered by many old Londoners like Lydia Bonnett.

I remember the first I heard of a place called Dunton. We were living in Hackney in 1924, and Dad came home from work one day and said Mr Sawyer, his foreman, had shown him an advert in the *Hackney and Kingsland Gazette* advertising plots of land there for five pounds a plot.

A plotland haven in the rural east. Lydia Bonnett (far right) and her family sit outside the bell tent in which they camped while building a shanty home in Dunton. It was one of the many thousands of do-it-yourself plotland houses built by poorer Londoners who couldn't afford a home in the suburbs

They both went out there at the weekend, and Mr Sawyer bought some but Dad couldn't afford it. Anyway, the next weekend Dad took Mum to Dunton and she fell in love with the place. Secretly she got a part-time job in a jam factory and saved up the money, then without Dad's knowledge she bought some plots next to the foreman's. The next time they went to Dunton, Dad was looking at these plots and Mum said, 'You would like some of those wouldn't you Bill?'

'Yes'.

So Mum said, 'Don't just stand there, get cracking, you want some posts and barbed wire, it's yours, I've just bought them.'

After this the whole family, we'd go to Dunton at weekends whatever the weather. We used to travel to Laindon railway station then walk. Dad bought a bell tent, and we used that in the summer. But when it was very cold a permanent resident there, a Mrs Taylor in First Avenue, used to let us sleep on the floor in her small bungalow. I loved sleeping in the tent and being out there – the fresh air, the dawn chorus, and the fields everywhere, that all made up for the lack of amenities. Mum would cook the meals on an oil stove.

Then as time went by Mum and Dad saved up a bit more money and brought out some building materials, and they started to build their little bungalow hoping when it was finished they would retire there. I've seen my mother with a pair of Dad's old trousers on, climb up a ladder to the roof and sit astride while Dad handed up the ridge tiles for her to fix and cement along the roof, those ridge tiles were very heavy. She was more at home with a trowel than a rolling pin! We all mucked in to help build it and we had many happy times there going out on Friday night and coming back late Sunday.

In the end the post-1945 planners cleared most plotlands away: Basildon New Town in Essex was built on the site of one of the largest of the settlements.

Most of the plotlands were, however, established well away from London's central suburban battle-ground, which still hugged the areas served by transport to the centre. It was in these non central areas that the LCC, with new money from the Labour Government of 1929, set out once again to look for land to build more cottage estates. In its first phase of 'out-county' building in the 1920s, the LCC had effectively been excluded from Hertfordshire, Kent and Surrey – the Becontree estate in Essex on London's eastern fringes, which were traditionally working class, had absorbed the single greatest concentration of the Council's building. Now, in the 1930s, despite the injection of funds from the Government, the LCC seemed doomed to be thwarted in their plans.

Political opposition to LCC encroachment on territory outside its boundaries had hardened, partly because there was a fear that the County Council was 'imperialist' and wanted to expand its territory to cover the whole of built-up London. The growth of London itself was also beginning to emerge as an issue, and the lack of planning of housing and transport in new developments was criticized. But, above all, a new programme of 'out-county' estate building was becoming a practical impossibility because of the extent of private development, as the LCC's valuer Frank Hunt reported in 1931:

Practically the whole of the developable land within a reasonable distance of railway stations had been so acquired and building operations thereon have either been completed or are well advanced. As a result of this demand, the price of such land as is now available has largely increased. It is also becoming increasingly difficult each year to secure sites suitable for the Council's requirements within a reasonable radius of the centre of London.

Hunt also anticipated that large landowners would now be unwilling to sell to the LCC, and got a rebuff from Lord Jersey when he approached him about his estate at Osterley Park on the LCC's behalf. Elsewhere, in Stanmore for example, any LCC bid for land was followed rapidly by a counter-bid from private interests. After a number of failed attempts, the LCC abandoned the suburbs to private enterprise, and turned its attention to re-housing slum dwellers in the centre of London.

'Up with the houses and down with the slums' was the Labour Party slogan in 1934, when for the first time the Party, led by Herbert Morrison, gained control of the LCC. But the houses they built were blocks of flats, giant developments described by a contemporary critic as 'worthy of Socialist Vienna'. Morrison said he still believed in the garden city, or satellite town ideal, but it was not practicable now.

But even when it turned its attention to inner London, the LCC was not able to build where housing was most needed. Many of the more radical boroughs like Bermondsey, Finsbury, Fulham and Woolwich had their own extensive housing programmes, and built blocks of flats themselves: they felt they did not need the LCC. Other boroughs were dominated by the Conservative Municipal Reform Party and would not allow the LCC in, or allowed only small-scale slum clearance, whether they were tackling the problem themselves or not. Whereas Bermondsey, a Labour-controlled council, built 2,700 dwellings between 1929 and 1938, the Conservative boroughs of Kensington, Paddington, Holborn and St. Marylebone built only

Part of the huge LCC-built China Walk Estate in Lambeth, completed in 1934. Opposition to cottage-estate building in the suburbs – which the middle classes felt to be their own territory – was one important factor which led the LCC to turn to building blocks of flats in inner London during the thirties

several hundred dwellings between them. The LCC was able to operate extensively in only a few places where there was no rival Labour programme, and opposition to their presence was weak. Almost half of the LCC's new tenement blocks were put up in only four boroughs: Southwark, Lewisham, Wandsworth and Lambeth, where there was land available at reasonable prices and sympathy from the local Labour parties.

So in the 1930s, the great bulk of the LCC's programme – as well as local authority housing as a whole – was in the form of flats, not houses. And it was nearly all within the LCC's own administrative boundaries. At the same time, far from seeking to build on the remaining open land of London's outer suburbia, Herbert Morrison resurrected the concept of the 'green belt'. This had originally been conceived as part of an entirely new structure for the capital, in which it would be ringed by satellite towns separated from the central core by countryside. Morrison's green belt was rather different – simply the preservation of the countryside which for one reason or another had survived the suburban building boom. The LCC offered county councils in these areas up to half the cost of acquiring land on the condition that it would remain open, and made available £2 million for this purpose. This proposition was taken up much more enthusiastically than previous attempts to re-house London's poor in such areas, and by 1939 about 13,000 acres had been acquired.

By then, however, much more dramatic political events were bringing the expansion of London to an end. With the declaration of war in 1939 the rate of building slowed down, grinding to a complete standstill a year later. Before this the threat of war and the concern about the vulnerability to air attack of such a vast capital had, in fact, provided useful propaganda for selling suburban houses. Builders advertised houses in so-called 'safety zones' with concrete shelters provided in back gardens. One enterprising builder in Southall supplied windows with seventeen hinges that could be tightened to form a seal in the event of a gas attack.

But it was the last gasp of the private building boom which had won the inter-war battle of the suburbs, and had covered the countryside around London with wave after wave of bricks and mortar. There was a growing realization that the spec'-built suburban dream had serious drawbacks – its haphazard growth was responsible for appalling land wastage, the destruction of valuable open spaces and traffic chaos. When, after the war was over, the Town and Country Act was passed in 1947, the spec' builder was to be controlled to a much greater extent by local and central government.

The IDEAL HOME

JUNE, 1935   ONE SHILLING NET

SUMMER IN HOUSE AND GARDEN

CHAPTER FIVE

IDEAL HOMES

THE FACT that semi-detached London built between the wars looks and feels so very different from the capital's Victorian and Edwardian fabric is a reflection not simply of developments in building styles influenced for instance by the garden city movement. This London could not have grown so rapidly had it not enshrined an evolution in lifestyle, which the speculative builder attempted to cater for in his efforts to sell houses, and the London County Council sought to encourage in the planning of its semi-rural cottage estates. For the way of life which emerged in the new London that was built in the 1920s and 1930s represented a clear break with the past for both middle- and working-class people.

The home, and in particular a new concept of the ideal home, was at the heart of this change in lifestyles. The Victorian middle classes did, of course, idealize the home and family life. But electricity, the radio, the reduction in the size of families and, as far as middle-class households were concerned, the disappearance of resident servants and the maid-of-all-work, gave the home a quite different atmosphere during the inter-war years. For the better-off Londoner, buying a home for the first time, the semi-detached house in the suburbs meant an essentially servantless house, wired for electricity, scaled down and re-arranged so that it could be run by the housewife on her own or with a minimum of outside help. One or two builders, falling behind the times, did design kitchens to be operated by servants, with no windows looking onto the garden – to ensure the privacy of the owners – only to find that this detail was quickly modified and a hole knocked in the wall to give the housewife a view while washing up. For some of the housewives who spent their lives in these suburban homes it was a dream come true, but others – as we shall see later – found it terribly lonely and depressing.

For poorer London families, moving from rented rooms to council house suburbia in Becontree or Downham meant a more comfortable home life with

Left: *Ideal Home* magazine cover for 1935. A host of such magazines fostered a suburban dream in which the modern woman was pictured as a housewife commanding a new servantless home and garden

greater living space, inside toilet and washing facilities and a garden. But – at least to begin with – the move also meant a weakening of community bonds between relatives and neighbours. The sense of community in the new working-class suburbs was often not as intense as it had been in the old inner-city areas, the new pub of the suburbs – whether a mock-Tudor roadhouse or a giant council estate tavern – was a less frequented and more family-centred sort of place, while the cinema and the radio set trends which transcended locality and class. Llewellyn Smith, editor of the *New Survey of London Life and Labour* compiled in 1929-30, was quite sure that because of the influence of the cinema local working-class accents were becoming less pronounced. And J.B. Priestley thought the same was true of personal appearance, with 'factory girls looking like actresses' – that is film stars. The old parochialism and the distinctive working-class image of poorer parts of London was breaking down.

In the forefront of the new lifestyle and the consumer revolution of this period – despite the fact that they represented a minority of the population – were the more prosperous middle classes living in the new suburbs. It was they who, by the mid-1930s, were buying electric cookers, vacuum cleaners, washing machines, electric fires and motor cars. The majority of the population had to wait until the affluence of the 1950s before they could begin to acquire these amenities. And it was those same middle classes who aspired to home ownership in the greatest numbers and who set the pattern for a more private suburban family life, revolving around the housewife.

In every period in London's history, old ways of life have existed alongside the new. But the contrast between emerging and disappearing lifestyles was particularly sharp in the inter-war years, partly because the pace of change was unusually rapid for one section of the community – the middle classes. Upper-class families, though perhaps living in slightly reduced circumstances, could still afford a much grander lifestyle in which domestic servants rather than machines did the work for them. For the many poorer working-class families living in the run-down villas deserted by the middle classes – in places like Finsbury, Hackney and Islington – home life was worlds apart from that in the new suburbs. It often meant sharing a house with one, two or several other families; terrible overcrowding, with all the beds jam-packed into the same room; humping water up the stairs from a standpipe in the back yard for all cooking or washing; and sharing an outside toilet with several other families. Here it was not so much a question of aspiring towards an ideal home but of struggling to keep any sort of home together at all.

The foundations of the new ideal home suburbia were laid before the First World War. The pioneers of this lifestyle came from an essentially new class of salaried person: there were the professionals whose ranks doubled nationally from 744,000 to 1,500,000 between 1911 and 1921; there was the rising number of civil servants brought about by the creation of new government departments such as the Ministry of Health and the Ministry of Pensions; and there were more clerical and managerial workers associated with the emergence of big business. London, as always, provided more work than anywhere else in Britain for this new class, and therefore supplied the new suburbanite in greater numbers.

In effect, as a group the middle class had become much more numerous since the Victorian era, but individually they were relatively less well off than their forebears. The great increase in taxation during the Great War, which remained in force in the 1920s, was one reason. But, more fundamentally, their sheer numbers ensured that they could not sustain the lifestyle of the Victorian person of private means. At the same time, the social aspirations of this middle-income group were moulded in an era when a technological revolution brought about by the development of electricity, and the advances of its great competitor, gas, affected the home as much as it did transport and industry. Home-ownership in itself encouraged a new attitude towards domesticity, while the slogan 'Let electricity be your servant' shifted the emphasis in social status from the employment of maids to the ownership of 'labour saving' devices, such as cookers, electric irons and vacuum cleaners.

Central to this series of social changes was the position of women, for it was the new housewife in command of the servantless house who was the key figure. And the decline of domestic service – which had been carried out almost exclusively by women – was intimately bound up with the new Ideal Home.

The story of the decline of domestic servants from the turn of the century is rather confused, because the official information on their numbers, and the kind of work they did, is difficult to interpret. Their numbers seem to have reached a peak around 1901, when there were nearly a quarter of a million women in service in the County of London – and certainly more if the whole built up area is included. Their numbers then began to decline, and the 'servant problem' – always a subject for debate in Victorian times – surfaced as a major social problem, becoming the subject of special government investigation. What confuses the issue here is the fact that 'living-in' servants were to some extent being replaced by part-time daily maids who lived in their own homes.

The reason for the decline in female servants is not properly understood, but almost certainly the drudgery of the work ensured that if women could find alternative employment, they would. The young maids-of-all-work had a particularly hard time, as the tragi-comedy of Lil Truphet's recollections of her tasks in New Cross before 1914 illustrate:

I was up at six in the morning and I didn't run in till ten at night, all for five bob a week. I was a slave to the missus. And the job I hated most, two or three mornings a week I used to have to vacuum certain rooms. But it wasn't a vacuum like we have today; it was like a bellows. I used to have to push the handle back and forwards with one hand, and with the other hand I used to have to put the nozzle round the carpet to pick up the dirt. And when each room was done I used to have to take the vacuum down, empty the dirt out of the paper bag and the missus would weigh it and look at it, and if I hadn't got enough dirt she used to make me go back and do it again. So I used to save bags of dirt in the pothouse. If I got a lot of dirt one day, I'd put some in there. So in the pothouse I had all different bags with different colours of dirt in them, taken from different carpets, and if I was a bit short, I'd get the right bag out and top up the dirt before I took it to show her. So I'd get the right quantity of dirt and that used to satisfy her.

Right: Lil Truphet as a maid-of-all-work in 1913, a job she loathed.

Opposite: Lil as a munitions worker (bottom row, second from right) in 1918. Her fiancé was so incensed at seeing her wearing trousers – a symbol of masculinity – that he ripped up her copy of this photograph and demanded her dismissal

Like a great many women of her generation, Lil Truphet was only too thankful when, in 1915, the trades unions and the government reluctantly agreed that they should be employed in munitions work and other formerly all-male occupations:

> Then when the jobs came up in the munitions, I couldn't get out quick enough. It was much more comfortable, it was more money – I was on two or three pounds a week – and with all the girls together we'd have singsongs and make friends, and it was more or less like a jolly party.

The experience of the freedom and camaraderie of the factory provided only a brief liberation, however, for the hundreds of thousands of women who ran the buses, became bank clerks, drove delivery vans and kept the home front going during the Great War. When men returned from the trenches, and the munitions industry closed down, many had to return to their old jobs or seek new ones in industries where male opposition was not strong enough to keep them out. The number of women domestic servants did decline in London, but not as sharply as many imagine. In the LCC area there were still

157,000 in 1921, and in the wealthier boroughs there was no dramatic disappearance of the cook and the 'tweeny'.

Working conditions had always been much better in richer households with a large staff than in the modest middle-class home, so perhaps this was the main cause. Wages for domestic service were also higher and could compete with factory work. In 1921, a comparison was made by the *New Survey of London Life and Labour* of domestic service in wealthy and middle-class boroughs. In the former, there were still 40 women servants per 100 families, a decline of a quarter since 1901, while in the latter there were only 13 per 100 families, representing a dramatic fall of 60 per cent in the same period. This was despite the fact that in the 1920s all kinds of pressures were put on working-class women to stay in domestic service. Former women servants could not get dole money from Labour Exchanges, and were excluded from unemployment insurance schemes, while training schemes for women were concentrated on domestic service.

The survey did not cover the new suburbs, but it was evident that by 1920 a large section of London's middle-class population had no servants at all. And perhaps the main reason for this was that while the middle classes had *increased* in numbers, domestic servants were slowly disappearing. Therefore a new middle-class household set up on marriage would have no expectation of employing a resident maid.

In this respect, the position of women after the war was crucial. In 1918 the Suffragette battle for the vote was partly won – in the sense that women over the age of thirty could now vote for the first time. But this new power was not matched by a liberation of women from a conventional view of their essential role in life. They had shown they could make bombs, repair aeroplanes, and accomplish just about any task the average man was asked to do. But that was not the point: all this was unwomanly, as Lil Truphet discovered even before her war work was over:

I was working on the bullets, then I was sent to the danger zone, and you had to wear a trouser suit, it was all khaki colour, and a bonnet cap. Well, all the girls got together and we had our photographs taken in our trouser suits, and my father was proud of it and he showed it to his friends. But my husband-to-be, he showed off, he didn't like me wearing trousers, he thought that was a disgrace.

The war was pretty well over by then and they were laying the women off. He came in and saw the overseer lady and said he didn't approve of me working there, it wasn't women's work. And he saw to it that I was dismissed, so I left about a fortnight after.

Although a Sex Disqualification (Removal) Act had been passed in 1919 to provide some protection for women in work, the general ethos was that they should know their place. Whereas working-class women were encouraged to return to domestic service (so as to solve the problems of the middle-class housewife), middle-class women were encouraged to stay at home. For example, in the 21 January issue of *The Times* in 1921 the continued employment of over two thousand women by the War Office was described as a 'monstrous injustice' – they should make way for men.

However, single women did manage to consolidate some gains that they had made during the war. This was particularly so in the new light engineering industries, and in clerical work. The number of women working in the Civil Service had risen to 102,000 from 33,000 during the war. But *married* women were expected to leave their jobs on or before their wedding day. Exactly how and why this bar on married women working came about is not clear. In some instances it was legalized; in the case of the Civil Service in 1921, for example, where single women actually supported the ban as it effectively reduced competition for their jobs. Similarly, in 1924, the London County Council determined that for women employees – which meant clerks, doctors, teachers, and so on – 'the contract shall end on marriage'.

Justification for the ban was usually couched in terms of the need for women to raise a family and keep the home happy, just as it might be today. And among middle-class and 'respectable' working-class men it became a matter of pride and status that their wife did not go out to work. It was also a way, of course, of ensuring that your dinner was ready when you got home. In the 1930s, Ivy Willis gave up her job as a bookbinder, even though she earned more than her husband and they needed the money:

My husband, just before we were married, said he felt I shouldn't go out to work. He felt he should be able to come home from work and find me there – not the little slave, because we both agreed on this – but I should be home ready to look after him and keep the home tidy. My boss was very angry when I said I would have to leave. He came down to see my husband and begged him to let me stay until somebody was trained to take my place, but my husband said 'no' he wouldn't allow me to go to work.

Every day I'd do my chores – cooking, cleaning and washing – and I used to watch for my husband coming home. Where I lived we could see the tram coming up the hill, and I used to watch for the tram coming at the usual time, and I'd run along the passage and open the door for him. He was what I call a steak and kidney pudding man, so I'd always make sure there was an enormous pie or pudding, and an apple pie or something like that for afterwards, on the table. I'd do everything myself, he didn't even wash up. He used to say he didn't keep a dog and bark himself, so he disagreed with doing anything, unless I was ill. Then he'd be very kind and do the work.

And Lil Rodgers, who worked as a Lyons 'Nippy' in the 1930s, was also pressurized into giving up her job:

I'd been courting for a little while and my husband and I decided to get married. Well, the hours I was working, sometimes it could be ten till six in the evening. If Hubby got home a bit early he didn't appreciate that, he'd be sitting there, because men didn't think much of doing their own meals in those days, and he used to say 'this is a fine time to come home'. And he kept getting annoyed, he used to say 'you give that bloomin job up', 'I'm going round my mum's for me Sunday dinners, I'm seeing nothing of you hardly' and 'I don't like the hours you're coming in of a nighttime'.

We quarrelled because I wanted to carry on working, we needed the money and I didn't have any children at that time. But after about three months he said to me 'either give the job up or give me up' which seemed a terrible thing to do in those days, and we discussed it and discussed it, and in the end I gave my job up. He said he found it beneath his dignity to have a wife working, and of course he wanted his meal on the table.

It was such social mores, rather than any legal disqualification, which appears to have been chiefly responsible for the fact that the great majority of married women did not work in the inter-war years, whether or not they had children. On the other hand, women were having fewer children; the birth-rate in Britain went down steadily from the late nineteenth century, spreading to all but the poorest working-class families by the 1930s. Why the birth-rate should have declined in this way, so that the average family size was reduced, from more than five children at the turn of the century to only two by the thirties, is not clear.

As early as the 1870s the better-off middle classes in Britain began to have fewer children, and one of the explanations given for this is that they were trying to maintain a kind of genteel lifestyle with carriages and servants on an income which was barely sufficient. Children also became more 'expensive' in that they were being educated to a higher level at greater cost. So from the start, the fall in family size was linked to an attempt to maintain a particular lifestyle. Similarly, in the twentieth century, it was the new middle class who had smaller and smaller families, and their decision to do so is probably connected with their desire to have a house of their own and to maintain the new suburban lifestyle, with mortgage repayments and consumer goods. Large families – except amongst the very wealthiest – were associated with poverty, and it was the poor who had most children in the 1930s. Though it is difficult to disentangle cause and effect, the creation of the Ideal Home, with an ideal 2.2 children, did go hand in hand and was part of the desire to enjoy a modest, well-ordered way of living on a small income. And this small family size was achieved by a large number of people by the 1930s, despite the fact that modern contraceptives were not widely used, and despite official campaigns encouraging bigger families, for there were fears that the population of Britain was going into decline.

This greatly reduced the burden of motherhood for most women so that by the 1920s, a new being – the lone housewife in her semi-detached home – was being created. A rash of new magazines sprang up, replacing those which had earlier catered for the Victorian lady administering a household staff of servants. The leader in the field in 1922 was *Good Housekeeping* which sold for a shilling. It had been developed in America, where there had always been a shortage of servants, and the concept of the 'housewife' had been created earlier. There followed among many other monthly magazines *Woman and Home* in 1926, *Wife and Home* and *Harpers Bazaar* in 1929. And in the 1930s, came the weekly magazines with higher circulations: *Woman's Own* in 1932, *Woman's Illustrated* in 1936, and *Woman* in 1937.

The tone and picture of life presented in these publications encouraged what *Woman's Life* in 1920 referred to as 'the return of the feminine type': 'The tide of progress which leaves woman with the vote in her hand and scarcely any clothes upon her back is ebbing, and the sex is returning to the deep, very deep sea of femininity from which her newly-acquired power can be more effectively wielded.'

In the home, this reincarnation of the feminine woman was to have a new source of power, which in time she was expected to wield almost like a

Below: The cover page of *Woman's Own* magazine, 1934, spelt out two important messages for the new woman. She was to aspire to beauty through fresh air and healthy exercise, and was encouraged to be a 'professional' housewife undaunted by technical tasks

Right: A thirties'-style National Building Society brochure. The image of a happy family enjoying the privacy of a beautiful back garden went to the heart of the dream of home-ownership

specialist domestic technician. It came from electricity and from gas; two industries which fought each other bitterly in the inter-war years to capture the attention and admiration of the woman in the servantless household.

By the 1880s, private homes were being lit by electricity, though the equipment was cumbersome and expensive, and as there was no centralized supply system, small generators had to be set up to provide the current. One such was installed in the 1880s in the Grosvenor Art Gallery in Bond Street by Sir Coutts Lindsay, and he called in the young Sebastian de Ferranti to develop a private distribution system which carried the excess power by overhead wires to more than three hundred customers, as far away as Regent's Park and the Law Courts.

There were other early electricity power schemes for domestic consumers, such as the small station built for the expensive block of flats, Kensington Court, in the 1880s, but before 1914 most electric power went into transport undertakings. Even in 1918, only about six per cent of homes were wired for electricity used almost exclusively for lighting. But in the next few years a very rapid expansion of the industry, both in the manufacture of equipment such as light bulbs, which became cheaper and more efficient, and the development of wiring systems, brought about a rapid rise in the use of electric power.

Prices and availability varied widely around the country, as the whole supply industry was run by private enterprise, or by local authorities, covering only a small patch of territory. However, the creation in 1926 of the Central Electricity Board with powers to pool the industry's resources brought some order to the chaos, and the systematic wiring of new houses was undertaken. Nearly all the semi-detached suburbs of London had electricity laid on, as well as many of the council cottage estates. But, as electricity was more expensive than coal or gas a great many poorer people could simply not afford to use it or have it installed, which was also costly.

The middle-class housewife was the chief target for promotional organizations such as the Electrical Development Association, which in the

A shop window display of the 1930s, trumpeting the advantages of electric fires. The electricity and gas industries fought a bitter battle for the hearts and minds of the suburban housewife during the inter-war years

An Ilford Borough Council
electricity van of the 1930s,
featuring the image of the modern
housewife that the council was
promoting. But, despite 'assisted'
wiring schemes and equipment hire
from local authorities, most
electrical appliances were beyond
the pocket of the majority of
working-class people

1920s and 1930s made a number of films extolling the wonders of the new
electric home. A silent film, *Edward and Edna*, made by the Association had a
young couple deciding to get married because the wife-to-be offered to run
the all-electric home without a servant.

There was, too, the Electrical Association for Women, founded in 1924,
and still offering courses in electricity for £5 a day sixty years later. It was set
up by Caroline Haslett, who had received an engineering training during the
First World War and wanted to consolidate the gains made by women
workers. In fact, this association perhaps inadvertently helped to promote not
the new woman engineer, but the housewife competent in the use of
electricity to run the home. For it was the electricity industry, and its efforts
to persuade women to use more and more electrical appliances in the home to
make housework easier, which was largely instrumental in creating a view of
the housewife as a home-bound 'professional'. *Good Housekeeping* called
housewives the 'craft workers of today'.

An American book, *Scientific Management in the Home* by Christine
Frederick, published in Britain in 1920, actually applied the 'time and motion'
studies of production-line industry to the kitchen, with diagrams setting out
the best layout of equipment. Research was carried out on the number of
hours the housewife spent on each task, and suggestions were made as to
how the workload could be reduced. Cleaning proved one of the most onerous
tasks, and the substitution of the coal fires and the coal range in the kitchen by
gas and electricity appliances greatly reduced the amount of dust in the house.

Electric irons cut down the time heating up the old models; vacuum cleaners saved brushing time; electric light meant the dust could be more easily seen, and could be cleared up later in the day.

In the creation of the Ideal Home, the gas industry fought electricity fiercely. Gas lighting in the nineteenth century had been by naked flame, and the gas mantle, which provided a brighter, more even light, was actually developed to compete with electric light bulbs. Electricity won the battle over lighting and ironing, but cheaper gas was favoured for cooking: by 1939 there were probably about eight or nine gas cookers for every electric cooker.

In fact, the electricity industry was more effective in promoting the ideal of the housewife running the all-electric home than in achieving it in the inter-war years. By 1939, of those houses – about two-thirds nationally – which had an electricity supply, nearly all would have electric lighting, 77 per cent an iron, 40 per cent a vacuum cleaner, 27 per cent electric fires, 16 per cent a kettle, 14 per cent a cooker, and less than 5 per cent a water heater. Generally speaking, electric appliances remained too expensive for the majority of people, despite the fact that both private companies and local authority suppliers – such as West Ham – had 'assisted' wiring schemes, and hired out equipment from their glossy showrooms.

Many modern electric appliances, then, were restricted to middle-class homes. But the suburban housewife's new 'professional' role not only involved taking over some or all of the tasks previously performed by a servant, but also raising standards of comfort and luxury in the home itself. Women's magazines encouraged a concern with style, which extended from

An inter-war suburban interior, showing some of the design elements popular amongst the middle classes. The fireplace with mahogany surround and tiled centrepiece is typical of the period

Right and opposite: Pages from a Wates' brochure for up-market thirties' houses. A luxurious modern bathroom was the jewel in the crown of the suburban middle-class home

buying 'tasteful' carpets, curtains and furniture, to experimenting with new foods. The overall effect aimed at – the good taste of the inter-war years – was a fusion of modern and historical styles. In the kitchen, new labour-saving equipment like an electric cooker would be set amongst cottage-style furniture, such as a scaled-down dresser. Similarly, in the living room modern elements like a three-piece suite with an Art Deco couch would be balanced by a Jacobean style table and chairs with 'twist' legs. And fireplaces, with their characteristic oak or mahogany surround and tiled centrepiece, would combine shapes which had historical overtones, perhaps of Aztec altars or Devon cottages, with Art Deco motifs; for instance, the ubiquitous fretwork sunblaze.

But the jewel in the crown of the suburban middle-class home was a luxurious or at least a comfortable bathroom. During the 1920s and 1930s the old-style bathroom with its cold white walls and mahogany furniture was transformed into the recognizably modern bathroom suite of today, with a coloured and enclosed bath, a heated towel rail and tiles replacing the old carpets and wallpaper. It has been argued that this great concern with the bathroom represented a reassertion of an old status symbol of the better-off. In the past the working classes could not afford plumbed-in baths and were always thought to smell, but in the inter-war years those who lived on cottage estates were provided with rather primitive, bare-walled bathrooms – thus the stress on luxurious bathrooms could be seen as a new attempt by the better-off to differentiate themselves from those beneath them on the social scale. Many, however, who lived in the run-down inner areas still had to make do with a zinc bath in front of the fire.

So the existed in London in the inter-war years an extraordinary range of lifestyles. For example, in the upper-middle-class household of the West End, Sunday lunch might still be served up by a maid and prepared by a cook. In her semi-detached, scientifically designed kitchen the suburban housewife probably produced the roast from her new enamel – therefore easier to clean – gas or electric cooker. And in the inner city slum areas of London, the working-class housewife might still be obliged to light a coal fire to cook, or the family might take the meal out to be cooked in the local baker's oven, a ritual Lal Brown recalls from Hoxton in the 1920s:

> We used to go down Essex Road Market on a Saturday night, half past nine, ten o'clock, and they'd be selling off meat cheap. They didn't have no ice blocks or fridges, they had to get rid of it cheap. So we'd buy a shoulder of lamb, for perhaps one and sixpence; they used to auction it off and you'd try and knock them down.

And then Sunday, you would prepare it, put your potatoes and your meat in a big dish, put your lump of fat on, cover it over, and take it down the street to the baker. He'd cook it for tuppence. We did that in the summer – not so much the winter, because in the winter you had a coal fire going anyway, so you could stick your dinner in the oven which was at the side of the fire, and it didn't cost you anything extra. But in the summer it was cheaper to take it to the bakers. And you'd have to wait a couple of hours before you went to collect, then there would be lots of women walking up and down the street with these big steaming dishes, and you'd lay the table with last week's *News of the World* – you mustn't read the *News of the World* because you weren't old enough – and then you'd get stuck in. That would be your best meal of the week.

While the middle classes went out to fashionable department stores to furnish their ideal homes, the poor would often kit themselves out on the cheap from the local street market. In fact, the centuries-old street markets actually grew in number in the inter-war years, so that by the late 1930s there were nearly a hundred of them in inner London – practically all to the East, in poor working-class districts like Brick Lane and Mile End Road and Portobello Road to the West. Over thirty thousand costermongers succeeded in scratching a living out of these colourful places. The markets promoted a great deal of recycling of furniture, carpets, curtains, ornaments, and so on. The contrast between these age-old market scenes with their bustle, bartering and repartee, and the affluent technological society of the 1920s and 30s could not have been greater. It was around this time that it became fashionable – because it was so 'different' – for better-off people to go rummaging around these places looking for bargains.

Mothers carrying their Sunday dinners through the streets of Limehouse in 1933 to have them cooked in the local baker's oven. This age-old practice remained common in inner areas like the East End until the Second World War because it was convenient and offered savings on fuel bills for poor families who had to make do with primitive cooking facilities

This more sociable and boisterous way of life, which survived in the run-down rented districts of inner London, was the very opposite of the new, ordered, and much more home-centred world emerging in the middle-class suburbs, which working-class people were urged to adopt on council cottage estates. The reaction of the first generation of cottage estate housewives to the sudden change from a communal life in the overcrowded streets and slums to a more comfortable and private life in the new working-class suburbs of Becontree, Downham and Watling was often mixed. On the one hand, they welcomed modern conveniences like an inside toilet and bathroom, more rooms, and a kitchen with running water as a godsend, releasing them from much of the drudgery of slum life. The greater privacy also reduced the danger of flare-ups over such matters as noise and dirt, an ever-present peril when families lived virtually on top of each other, and shared basic cooking and toilet facilities.

But at the same time many experienced a psychological shock when they were exported to the suburbs, and quickly discovered that their new, more private family life could have practical drawbacks as well. For tenement-living in places like Bermondsey and Poplar fostered, over the years, all sorts of communal bonds – looking after neighbours' children, borrowing sugar, running errands, and perhaps going on an annual charabanc outing to Southend. And in the old inner-city areas whole families – mothers, grans, uncles, cousins, and so on – often lived within walking distance and would see each other almost every day. All this added up to a mutual support system of and for the poor. This was disrupted, at least temporarily, in the suburbs, where everybody was to begin with a stranger in a more isolated environment. Those who were hit the hardest tended to be women who came from large families, or who had lived with their parents. Mary Budd was one of fourteen children who lived with their parents in two rooms in Notting Dale, one of the poorest areas of North Kensington. When she got married and moved out to the Watling Estate in 1928, she remembers: 'I never stopped crying to begin with, it was so lonely, there was nobody to talk to, I'd just stand and stare out of the window.'

Other problems, too, faced residents of council cottage estates: the rents were sometimes too high for families to afford; shops were few and far between, which meant a long hike to get the groceries; transport facilities into town and across the estate were often inadequate and expensive; and there were few of the social activities and entertainments, like the pub and the music hall, that were on the doorstep in central London. For these sorts of reasons there was, in the early years of some estates, an incredibly high turnover of tenants. For those who moved away – like Doris Scott, who spent two years on the Dagenham Estate between 1937 and 1939 – the Ideal Home they had dreamed of in the country proved a bitter disappointment, making the advantages of city life doubly attractive:

I hated it, living out there altered your whole way of life, really. The streets were very long and you had to trek half a mile or a mile to the nearest shops. Well, I didn't approve of that, that was too far for my liking. Especially after I'd been used to living quite close to a market in Canning

Town, that was much cheaper and more convenient. And it was terribly lonely and boring, it seemed so dead. I was used to being with people all the time, and I used to know most of the people in our street. But out on the estate the lights seemed to go out at eight o'clock everywhere and there was nothing to do. Another thing was you spent so much time travelling and it took your husband so long to get home, that by then it was too late to do much, like in the way of going out for a drink. In any case the pubs out there were very few and far between.

And where I'd lived before, Mother was on hand to babysit. I remember I spent so much time going back on the bus to see mother and my old friends that she said 'you might as well live here'. So that's what we did, we went back to rooms in Canning Town. I wasn't the only one that did, lots couldn't settle, droves of us went back. We were glad to get back to civilization.

To what extent the Ideal Home of the middle-class housewife was a lonely place which led to a sort of suburban neurosis in the living-rooms of Croydon, Ruislip and Wembley is a matter of some conjecture. There was a social life of sorts for women in the better-off suburbs, usually centring on coffee mornings, tennis clubs, amateur dramatic societies and residents' associations. But for the young mother in her semi-detached, whose husband left on the 8.05 and arrived back on the 6.25, the Ideal Home could turn into a prison. For practically everything revolved around her home, her garden and her family, which meant that few friendships were usually made beyond immediate neighbours and relatives. Since the 1960s there has been a revolt, especially amongst feminists, against this sort of isolated, suburban existence. But in the 1930s, the ideology of the Ideal Home reigned supreme, and the sacrifices of career and social life it involved for women were rarely questioned. As a result many middle-class women – certainly those

Cleaning the family Morris 8. A Sunday spin out into the countryside or down to the coast was one of the new family recreations that became increasingly popular amongst the middle classes during the thirties

interviewed for this book and television series – felt fairly content and fulfilled in their routine suburban lifestyle. Possibly because they themselves would often have been brought up in a private family atmosphere, they seem to have suffered less anguish than their working-class contemporaries in adjusting to the new home-centred rhythm of suburban life.

The increasing home-centredness of life in the 1920s and 1930s was encouraged by a number of changes in leisure activities and entertainments in the inter-war years. One of the most conspicuous changes was the decline in drinking after the First World War. This was partly due to higher prices of beer and new opening and closing time restrictions. In addition, improvements in housing conditions were making the home a more attractive place to spend an evening in – prior to this many working-class people had been regulars at the local pub partly because it was warmer, more comfortable and more spacious than their overcrowded homes. But this change was also partly engineered by authorities like the LCC and licensing magistrates who, in an attempt to defeat the problems of crime and violence associated with heavy drinking, hardly built any pubs at all on the new council estates.

Whereas in central London there was an average one pub for every 500 people, on the Becontree estate just six pubs were provided to cater for 120,000 – a ratio of one pub per 20,000 people. On the Downham Estate there was just one pub – even though it was the biggest in Britain – for the entire estate of 35,000 people. And the pubs themselves tried to encourage drinking habits that differed from the raucous, rough-and-ready pub scenes of inner London. They encouraged the sale of soft drinks and a family atmosphere, and most of the space was devoted to areas where families could eat, drink and be entertained together. Indeed, they weren't actually called pubs at all, but refreshment houses, and they were huge, relatively impersonal places lacking the cosy intimacy of the old smoky bars.

George Orwell commented on this change in *The Road to Wigan Pier*:

As for pubs, they are banished from the housing estates almost completely, and the few that remain are dismal sham-Tudor places fitted out by the big brewery companies and very expensive. For a middle-class population this would be a nuisance, it might mean walking a mile to get a glass of beer; for a working-class population, which uses the pub as a kind of club, it is a serious blow at communal life.

The Downham Tavern had no stand-up bars when it was first built – an LCC member had said he was against 'perpendicular drinking' – and offered a waiter service, with a staff of thirty-two in 1932. Many working-class Londoners found it all a bit of a nuisance, especially when they had to tip the waiter to make sure he would answer their call for drinks during the evening, as Bill Peek recalls:

You couldn't go to the bar yourself, you had to call the waiter. And they were all in monkey suits, bow-tie and so forth. And there were liveried men outside to open the door, 'Good evening Sir. Good evening, madam',

The Downham Tavern, one of the new breed of giant-sized pubs built on cottage estates, some of which had no stand-up bars to begin with so that drinks had to be ordered through waiters. Pubs like this tried to encourage a respectable, family atmosphere and to control what was thought to be the excessive drinking habits of working-class people moving out from central London

trying to make working men things they were not. I thought it was an imposition, you couldn't go and get your own pint, you had to wait for the waiter and if you couldn't give him a half penny or a penny tip, you had to wait until he served all his regulars from whom he got the tips.

All this, plus the fact that to get a pint you could easily find yourself walking one or two miles each way to the nearest pub, must have provided a powerful incentive to stay at home. For many, home-centred activities like gardening began to take over from drinking and socializing in the pub as the main leisure pursuit.

The cinema, of course, did not directly encourage a home-centred way of life. But the entertainment it provided, with its celebration of romantic love and the American Dream, helped to reinforce the new aspiration towards family activities and consumer comforts. It was the sort of place courting couples, husbands and wives, or entire families might go for a night out. Even the poor were greeted by uniformed doormen and shown by usherettes to their seats in palaces decked out in as exotic a style as any opera house.

The cinema had arrived in Britain and become immensely popular before the First World War, by which time there were reckoned to be up to three hundred picture houses in Greater London. All films were, of course, silent, accompanied in the local flea pit by a piano, or by full orchestra in the more expensive West End palaces. But from the beginning it was noticeable that these new forms of entertainment were sited outside the traditional theatrical centre of London. Whereas many of the old theatres and music halls had been concentrated in the central areas, the enormous new picture palaces which were built in the 1920s and 1930s rose up all over London. In Brixton, Tooting, Kilburn and Hackney, for instance, cinemas looking like modern cathedrals dwarfed the suburban buildings around them. These cinema chains of Astorias, Granadas, Gaumonts, Odeons and Roxys, showing films made in Hollywood, provided entertainment on a much cheaper and grander scale than ever before.

They quickly outstripped the theatre and the music hall. Some of the new cinemas had vast seating capacities of up to 4,000 and by 1929 there were 266 of them in the LCC area alone with accommodation for 268,000 people. In six typical working-class boroughs – Stepney, Shoreditch, Bethnal Green, Poplar, Southwark and Bermondsey – with a combined population of one million, there were in 1929 only five theatres and music halls (compared with eighteen in 1981) but fifty-nine cinemas. This new form of entertainment, which could be enjoyed for up to four hours at a stretch without a trip to the West End, was the cheapest available, 'truly the poor man's theatre' as the *New Survey* put it. The price of cinema seats, at around sixpence, matched the cheapest music hall of the day, and was a third or less of the price of the theatre. For sixpence people of all classes could experience an extraordinary fantasy world: they could admire the grandiose and opulent designs of the cinema interiors, and they could enjoy the glamour of the Hollywood stars. One of the most lavish interiors was the Tooting Granada – which is now a Bingo Hall – with its gigantic foyer designed like a medieval baronial hall, a marbled columned hall of mirrors, and a 3,500-seater auditorium in a Venetian Gothic style complete with chandeliers and rows of cloistered arches lining the walls.

There were from time to time panics about the morally dangerous effects of the cinema. It was blamed for encouraging people to buy American rather than British products, for provoking unbridled sexual desire and reckless violence, and it was even suggested that darkness in cinemas might produce moral dangers – particularly in the back row. Most of these fears were almost certainly unfounded but the cinema, by bringing Hollywood stars to a vast audience, helped to create an image of womanhood which was taken up by women's magazines of the period. Together the magazines and the movies brought the feminine fantasy all the way back home to the housewife, who was now not only expected to be a 'craft worker', but one modelled in the fashion of film stars.

One of the few entirely new influences on people's lives in the twenties – the radio – also encouraged a new home-centredness and provided an alternative to the boisterous life of the public house and the streets. When the British Broadcasting Company, a consortium of five manufacturers, began to broadcast in 1922, there were 36,000 licence holders, pioneers from the early days of amateur enthusiasts. The first commercial sets were primitive and mostly battery-operated, but the technology improved very rapidly. By 1931 4.3 million people had radio licences, and by 1939 the figure had more than doubled to 9 million. Just about everyone in Britain listened to the radio.

It is interesting that as an entirely new product, the radio – or the wireless as it was known at the time – had to be designed without any reference to an

A London suburban family listens to the results of the 1931 election on the radio, or the wireless as it was known at the time. The radio encouraged a new home-centredness, providing a form of home entertainment that was more continuous and absorbing than anything available before

older appliance. This raw piece of technology brought an alien element into cottage-style homes. To overcome this, some manufacturers tried to blend it into the scenery by disguising it as a drinks cabinet or hiding it in a chest. Other manufacturers brought in a modernist Art Deco style, employing well-known designers, some of whom decorated the speaker surrounds with sun motifs. Radio sets therefore brought design into some people's homes for the first time. But much more than that, radio provided a form of home

entertainment that was more continuous and absorbing than anything available before.

The BBC – which became the Corporation in 1927 – attempted under Lord Reith to instil a 'high' culture and a pious Christian morality through the new medium. On Sunday classical church music was broadcast. It was the commercial stations, broadcasting from Europe – Radio Luxembourg, Radio Normandy, and many others – who could capture an audience longing for some livelier entertainment. The commercial stations survived on advertising and sponsored programmes, which meant that they were promoting products – and what better medium for reaching the housewife than the radio in her own home. Advertisements for Johnson's wax polish, Palmolive soap, Heinz beans and the like helped to reinforce the 'housewifely' way of life. Children were catered for too, with the very first recorded programme broadcast by Radio Luxembourg: 'The Ovaltiney Concert Party' sponsored by Wonderfood's, the makers of Ovaltine. It first went out in 1934, and from it grew the League of Ovaltineys, a nationwide band of five- to fourteen-year-olds, who were sworn to do the things their parents told them, to study hard at school, to eat the things their mother wanted them to eat, and to drink Ovaltine every day. There were over one million Ovaltineys by 1938, huddled round their radio sets and taking down coded messages which, when deciphered, told them to help their mothers, and such like. The main target area was the new, middle-class suburbia, where good little children might be raised – and who might encourage their mothers to buy Ovaltine.

In its own way the BBC also helped to build up the sense of homeliness with programmes about things to do about the house, and with gardening talks given by Mr Middleton. He enjoyed a personal following of millions and gardening – both in the middle-class suburbs and in the new cottage estates, which gave many working-class people a piece of land to tend for the first time in their lives – became one of the most popular pastimes of the inter-war years. The gardens enjoyed by home-owners in the semi-detached suburbs were, however, often substantially bigger than those provided for council tenants. And although the council house garden was sometimes just a scaled-down version of its private counterpart, there were important differences.

What characterized the middle-class suburban garden most of all was a concern with the privacy of the family. At the front the barrier to outsiders were merely symbolic. Most commonly it comprised a privet hedge nestling behind a low brick wall topped with iron chains – which was suggestive perhaps of the drawbridge and the castle wall. But at the back seclusion was considered even more important, especially in the area close to the house, and the customary five-feet-high fences erected by builders would often be raised by the householder to a height of eight feet or more, using open work trellis trained with roses. The back garden would usually be divided into two zones, the lower end being devoted to vegetables – fresh food for the family – while the half closest to the home would have a lawn, flower beds and borders, and perhaps a rockery. Suburban couples cultivated in this part of the garden a sort of tidy, miniaturized version of natural beauty, but they also ensured there was space for the children to play, for the dog or the cat to mark out its territory, for mum and dad to sunbathe, and for the family washing to be hung up. And the finishing touches which gave the garden that 'olde worlde', natural feel – perhaps a symbolic escape from the ever-changing inter-war world of big business and scientific advance – were crazy paving, a bird table, a sundial, and a cluster of red hatted gnomes wielding axes or fishing rods.

In the working-class garden this sort of privacy was often not possible or even aspired to. The gardens were smaller, so that a conversation could be held with somebody two houses away. And high fences were considered an unnecessary expense – most of the money was needed for more essential items like food and the rent. In the council garden there would commonly be a small lawn, flower bed and vegetable patch, but it was all scaled down with few of the frills which graced the miniature 'estates' of semi-detached and detached homes.

A Mass Observation survey into housing, part of which asked 'gardenless' working-class people in North London what they would do with a garden if they had one, gives a good indication of the uses gardens were put to on council estates in the inter-war years. Their answers, listed in order of preference, were growing vegetables, growing flowers, growing 'things', keeping chickens, relaxation, children to play in, nothing, drying washing, having a dog kennel, keeping rabbits, and keeping pigs. Their preferences show how the keeping of livestock – which provided a cheap supply of fresh food, particularly useful in hard times – was probably more important than it is today. The LCC, in fact, had rules preventing the keeping of livestock, but these only seem to have been imposed when animals became a nuisance. Rather than a manicured suburban garden, many working-class people favoured a 'take us as you find us' farmyard style. Doris Hanslow, whose father was a taxi driver, and who moved with her family from Bermondsey to the Downham estate in the mid-twenties, recalls:

When we first moved out to Downham, we used to invite all our old friends from Bermondsey down for the weekend to stay. Sometimes there would be twenty-five of us in the one house, and it would be treated like a mini-holiday. It was a big attraction then, our friends were thrilled to bits with our lovely new house, and so were we. We'd give them a guided tour, first they wanted to go upstairs and look at the bathroom and toilet, because no-one had got one you see, and they couldn't get over how lovely it was.

Then they'd see all the rooms, there was so much room to move in them, and the garden, that was my father's pride and joy. And they'd all have to see the animals we were caring for. There was the goat we had. My dad always went up and brought the goat in to introduce it, and of course there used to be screams of delight and 'get away from me'. Then we had a pigeon that had broken its leg, and Dad had put a little splint on it; there was Gertie the duck, she just used to follow us in and out all the time; and the most horrible cockerel that used to go for you if you tried to feed it. It was like being out in the country, because there were fields at the back of us in those days, and we'd often go for walks and come back and have a sing-song in the evening around the piano.

So the new suburban London which grew up between the wars did, in a great many ways, represent a new lifestyle. Not everyone could enjoy it, and not everyone wanted it, but it marked a sharp break with the past. This was most true for the middle-class owner-occupier family and, in particular, the housewife in her servantless home. The municipal suburbia drew in people with less money to participate in the new consumer lifestyle and less inclination to hide away in Arcadia. As they became more firmly rooted in the suburbs the community bonds which had been severed in the slums were to some extent restored. Relatives moved out to be close to each other, neighbours built up community networks, and children – unlike many of their middle-class counterparts – played on the streets. Nevertheless, their lifestyle was more home-based than it had ever been before.

CHAPTER SIX

A
BRAVE
NEW WORLD

M OST OF US don't readily associate things like parks, playing fields and council flats with an idealistic vision of the future. Today they often look rather shabby, and are so firmly embedded in London's landscape that we take them for granted as an ordinary and mundane part of our everyday life. Yet the rusted swing in a council playground, the sadly neglected lido and the crumbling council block are relics of a period when municipal idealism was at its height. An effort was made to build a brave new world that would rise out of the slums of Victorian inner London. Its highest aim was to stamp out the appalling poverty, disease and degradation that persisted in the heart of the Empire, and to make run-down boroughs like Bermondsey, Battersea and Hackney beautiful places to live in.

The 1920s and 30s saw the convergence of two ideals – a romantic ideal of a lost rural England, and a faith in planning and scientific advance. The worship of fresh air, fitness, sunshine and village life has a long history, which embraces William Morris and the garden city movement, but it really flowered in London from around the turn of the century. You can see evidence of it everywhere: cottage-style houses, tree-lined roads, LCC parks, cricket pitches, lidos, and so on. This old ideal became fused with a much more modern faith in the power of science and of the state. Gas, electricity, medical advances and modern equipment could, it was believed, if harnessed properly, provide much greater comfort, health and happiness for all. What emerged was a sort of municipal socialism, an embryonic welfare state, in which the local council took far more responsibility for matters of health and housing, and ran services – at least in theory – for the good of the local community.

Special attention was paid to the well-being of children: they were the hope for the future, the citizens of tomorrow's London. The inter-war years saw the development of free school milk, regular dental and health check-ups and treatment, and solarium sessions in places like Bermondsey, to boost up children's Vitamin D intake, which it was feared might drop because the London 'pea soupers' and the tightly packed housing in poor areas often prevented the sun's rays from filtering through. And there was swimming in pure water lidos and open-air lessons and entertainments in London's parks, and special schools for the sick and the blind.

Many of these changes grew out of an anger with the Dickensian world of rickety, bare-footed urchins, stinking tenement slums and prison-like workhouse regimes, which survived into the twentieth century in inner London. In the past philanthropy and the Poor Law had been two of the main forces grappling with the problems of poverty and disease in the capital. An essentially Victorian heritage of philanthropic dwellings for the working classes, voluntary hospitals, workhouses and the like, still dominated public provision for the poor in the pre-welfare state world of 1914.

Previous pages: A banner proclaims Poplar Council's crusade for its people at the opening of the King George V Dock in 1921. A new wave of post-war unemployment reduced many families to a bread-line existence in what was already the poorest area in London

But this was gradually being overhauled and the new faith in planning, in science and in municipal socialism was given a tremendous impetus by the collective refusal of increasing numbers of working-class people to put up with poverty after the war. There was a whole constellation of forces behind this change in attitudes. An awareness by working-class people of the important part they had played in the Great War, the promises of politicans to create a better world, and the extension of the franchise which gave many men and women in London the right to vote for the first time in 1918, all combined to create a strong demand for social reform. Much of this anger and idealism was channelled into the Labour Party, which by the early 1920s was becoming an important political force in the capital, especially at a local level. Socialist candidates were particularly successful in working-class areas and the Labour Party gained control for the first time in places like Poplar, Bethnal Green, Bermondsey and Hackney, with dustmen, postmen, general labourers and the like, who had little or no formal education, being elected as councillors and mayors.

In each borough the Labour Party set about creating what they believed might become a municipal utopia. After the war there was little conception that a Socialist majority in Parliament could be achieved in the foreseeable future, so with urgent social problems to deal with, it made sense to these town hall visionaries to aim for a local revolution in health and housing, using what powers they had. Public parks were created or given a face lift with landscaped gardens, swimming pools and lidos; some of the worst slums were knocked down and in their place garden village estates and later modern blocks of flats were created; and local health services were improved. A characteristic campaign of the early twenties was Labour's mission to 'Beautify Bermondsey'. It was initiated by the council, who provided free bulbs and seeds for local residents, and was so successful that after six years of Labour rule there were hundreds of window boxes blossoming with colour, and trees could be seen in almost every street and alley. For a time the council even attached pots of hanging flowers to lamp posts.

Building the 'New Jerusalem', however, cost a lot of hard cash and Labour councils ran into trouble with the LCC, which until 1934 was controlled by the essentially conservative Municipal Reform Party – and with the government itself, over their spending on local services. In the early twenties some of them were prepared to defy the law if necessary, and their zeal to form what was then seen as a revolutionary local state led them to be dubbed 'Little Moscows' in the press. The most dramatic revolt occurred when Poplar took the lead in transforming the whole basis of the Poor Law and the workhouse system in London.

To understand what this rebellion was all about, we must first briefly look at how the Poor Law worked and the terrible suffering it could cause to those forced to resort to it for relief. In London, as elsewhere, welfare hand-outs and help for the aged, the poor, the sick and the unemployed, were largely administered by the Poor Law Boards of Guardians, of which there were twenty-seven elected in the LCC area. The poor relief they provided varied enormously from one area to another, but generally in London immediately after the Great War they offered a spartan and subsistence form of welfare, which was invariably administered in a punitive way. The poorest widows, unmarried mothers, orphans, the chronically sick, and the disabled were incarcerated in workhouses where they were often subjected to a harsh regime which had changed little since Charles Dickens attacked the system in his novel, *Oliver Twist*. Able-bodied men were given 'outdoor relief', whereby they could continue living with their families only if they completed a 'labour test' which usually involved eight hours of stone-breaking in the labour yard in return for a small payment or food tickets. The Poor Law authorities had for almost a hundred years been deliberately cultivating a mean image for the workhouse in order to deter what they saw as society's 'lame ducks', who, it was thought, would take advantage of a cosy berth rather than do an honest day's work. This severity was reinforced by the self-supporting principle whereby relief was financed out of the local rates – here was a powerful inducement to keep costs as low as possible.

The system was in most parts of London antiquated and inadequate at the best of times, but when a new wave of unemployment hit the capital in the early 1920s, it was overwhelmed. There was, in fact, a government insurance scheme, but payments were small and could only be claimed for short periods. In any case, the vast majority of the unemployed were ineligible for the benefits. So, thousands of respectable families who had never before contemplated the idea of going to the Poor Law Guardians suddenly found themselves at the mercy of the Poor Law during the slump of the twenties.

Chopping wood in a London workhouse. Harsh Dickensian conditions in workhouses made them a source of terror for poor people, and a prime target for the reforms of radical councils in the inter-war years

One group who were hit particularly hard by the severity of the Poor Law was single-parent families and their children. Boards of Guardians had for many decades adopted a policy of breaking up such families and dispatching the children to orphanages, so that they would not be such a burden on the rates. In the post-war years there was a big increase in single-parent families due to the death of one of the parents, most often as a result of the war or the killer 'flu epidemic which followed it. Most of the guardians, with little money to play with, reacted in a traditionally harsh way, showing little of the concern for children and family welfare which was to emerge in London in the 1930s.

Many Londoners have stories about their mothers going to the Board of Guardians, only to be offered relief on the condition that their children were taken away and brought up in an orphanage. This threat often sparked off remarkable struggles to hold families together, particularly in the immediate post-war years. Doris Scott, whose father was drowned one foggy night in the Thames, found that she, as the eldest daughter, had to make almost as many sacrifices as her mother to save their Canning Town family from being dispersed:

> Our Mum, with myself trailing behind, called on the Board of Guardians to try to get outdoor relief. Well, when we went in, it was a kind of board, and Mother had to stand on the carpet in front of them while I was left holding our dear new-born baby in my arms – we'd left the other four at home – and we waited for the verdict.
>
> 'Madam,' announced a bloody bloke like Scrooge, 'we will give you food tickets but not enough to keep your six children. You may keep the new baby in your own care as it's breast fed, but your eldest child – that was me – must leave school straightaway to earn some money. The four other children will be sent to an orphanage.'
>
> Mother said 'Orphanage? I couldn't think of parting with any of my children. I don't care if I have to scrub floors and work all hours, I won't part with my children.'
>
> So off we went. From then on Mother scrubbed floors for Jewish plutocrats, and did sweatshop tailoring, anything to keep us kids all together. My sentence was to leave my lovely school almost at once, which really upset me. I'd won a scholarship to a Central School and I used to cry myself to sleep at the thought of leaving. A lady who lived in our street said, 'I'll speak for her, get her a job in the jam factory.'
>
> The factory was just across the road from us and the advantage was I'd have no fares to pay. So, I started work in the jam factory, no less, I got nine shillings and ninepence a week.

Anne Hitchins, a young mother in Limehouse, was forced to resort to more desperate means to keep her children:

> I did apply for assistance, and when someone came to interview me, they told me I'd have to put the children away in a home before they'd give me any money. But I didn't want to lose my children, my children were my treasures. I had a baby that would have been about six months and a boy of

two, and I was in such a quandary, I didn't know what to do, you see. I told the person to get out, so he said, 'What are you going to do, start stealing?' I said 'No'.

Then I thought, which way can I turn. I knew that my children were hungry and I swore that my children would never go hungry again, and no one was going to take them away from me. So, after I'd put them to bed I went out and sold myself for just a few shillings. I went to an all-night café, I bought a tin of Nestlé's milk for my baby and a sponge cake and some ham sandwiches for my boy, and I woke them up. And I gave my little boy a ham sandwich and when he got half way through he said, 'Mummy, I don't want any more' and this picture is engraved in my memory.

Then I started doing it as a regular thing. I used to go up to the café just up the street, and there would be sailors, a lot of them were Chinese sailors, or American tourists, or businessmen. They'd come up and speak to the children, I'd get into conversation, and that's how I used to meet them. Some would be regulars, boyfriends, and they'd be kind to me. I'd take them back to my place, or arrange to meet them there. I'd always do it in the other room when the children were asleep. Some would be a pound or two pounds. See, the more money I got the less I'd do it. They'd always have to pay first, because beforehand they'd promise you the world, then when they'd had what they wanted it was bye, bye. I was caught like that.

The idealistic Labour councillors who swept to power after the war were not prepared to accept this sort of harsh treatment of the poor, and the misery and desperation which followed from it. In some areas like Poplar they were winning control of the Board of Guardians as well as the council – sometimes the same people were elected on both bodies – and they took immediate action. In Poplar they fixed relief scales which were above those offered by most other guardians, and they refused to impose a maximum family rate – standard practice in most other areas – which meant that the 'hand out' was often inadequate to support a large family. Because of this rule a large single-parent family in Poplar could survive fairly comfortably on the Poor Law. Elsewhere, the family may well have broken up, the children going to an orphanage.

But all this benefit had to be paid for out of the local rates and by 1921, with increasing unemployment forcing more than one in five of Poplar's breadwinners to claim relief, this was becoming a crippling burden to the local people. For Poplar, a dock area overshadowed by railway goods yards and gasworks, and cut through by canals bordered with wharves and warehouses, was the poorest borough in the capital. The councillors led by George Lansbury, the future Labour Party leader, refused to put pressure on the guardians – who were overspending – to reduce their relief rates. Instead they made a stand to reform the whole rating system. They decided not to levy rates due to the LCC, the Metropolitan Police or the Metropolitan Asylums Board, until rate equalization was brought in whereby richer boroughs like Westminster and Kensington paid their fair share towards the social costs of poverty and unemployment.

These were a new breed of politician, invariably working-class men and women, born and bred in the areas they served, whose life and political work

were deeply rooted in their local community. They commanded much respect in Poplar, and they quickly became local heroes when, after a long legal battle, thirty of them, including the mayor, were sentenced to be imprisoned. Their arrests were announced in advance in the Press and were used by the Labour Party to whip up local popular feeling by organizing peaceful demonstrations whenever and wherever the arrests took place. When Poplar's five women councillors were arrested at the town hall, they were driven at walking pace down the East India Dock Road to Holloway, escorted by a procession of 10,000 local sympathizers.

The revolt became front-page news in national newspapers throughout the autumn of 1921, and was referred to sneeringly as 'Poplarism'. *The Times* denounced it as a 'revolutionary movement for the equalisation of wealth'. Yet, remarkably, in the face of hostility to their actions the Poplar councillors triumphed, the Conservative central Government and the LCC dropped all charges against them and they were released from prison after six weeks amidst great victory celebrations. The people of Poplar's support was probably the key factor in the victory, for the government's trump card, the appointment of officers to collect the outstanding rates from local residents, would have been met by a rent strike organized by a Tenant's Reform League in which thousands had quickly enrolled. Also, the government was well aware that other Labour councils, like Bethnal Green and Shoreditch, were considering direct action on rate equalization, and to penalize them would

One of the many demonstrations in support of the rebellious Poplar Council by local workers and trade unions in the summer of 1921. They had staged a rate strike, refusing to make payments to authorities like the LCC until rate equalization was brought in, whereby richer boroughs would pay towards the costs of poor relief

Poplar's convicted women councillors being driven at walking pace down the East India Dock Road to Holloway Prison, escorted by a procession of 10,000 local sympathizers. The extraordinary support the people of Poplar gave to their councillors paved the way for a victory for London's working class and a triumph over the government

have further disrupted local government and might trigger violent resistance. The end result was that the richer London boroughs were forced to contribute far more substantial sums to help pay for unemployment and deprivation in poor areas like Poplar.

Similar battles to improve welfare services and living standards were fought by rebellious London Labour parties in the early 1920s. The Poplar Guardians paid relief rates over and above a new maximum fixed by the Ministry of Health and, after an official investigation, continued to defy government orders, spending £2,000 a week above their limit. After twelve months the guardians faced a surcharge of £110,000, but no attempt was made to retrieve the money. The Poplar Guardians also openly made illegal unemployment benefit payments to local men involved in the unofficial London dock strikes of the summer of 1923. Likewise, the Labour councils in Bermondsey, Battersea, Bethnal Green, Poplar and Woolwich resisted strong government pressure to reduce the wages they paid to council workers, which they generously fixed at about £4 5s. for skilled workers and £4 for the unskilled – this compared very favourably with wage rates in the private sector. Dustmen in run-down inner London were in the early 1920s among the best paid in the country. In 1925, though, after five years of what the government saw as 'overpayments', the councils were forced by the Law Lords to lower their wage rates. Eventually, from 1929, central government began to take away Poor Law Boards' powers, and created a new system of public assistance committees.

The kind of direct action in which the Poplar councillors engaged, challenging the authority of central government, was quite common in the twenties. In a rather different guise, it came to a head in 1926 with the General Strike. For nine days in May, a substantial section of London's working class came out as part of a national strike to give industrial muscle to a long-standing dispute in which miners were resisting a wage cut. On the surface the strike was all about solidarity and sympathy with the miners. But underneath it was a battle between the classes, in which the well-to-do were holding off the demands of a Socialist-led working class for a more equal society in which they had a bigger slice of the economic cake. Many people thought, at the time and since, that this was a potentially revolutionary situation. At the very least it was a very important test case, for if the government and employers had caved in, many more workers would have joined the queue for wage increases and better conditions.

The TUC's plan was to bring out one section of industry at a time, reaching a crescendo after a few weeks that would force the government into submission. Some of the main first-line industries called out on 3 May were transport, printing and electricity – all important employers in London. Support for the strike was strong in these three industries. The London dockers came out en masse and huge gatherings of strikers, supported by Port of London Authority clerical and supervisory staffs, immobilized the docks for several days until the government moved in troops and forced the unloading of ships with machine-guns trained on pickets. London's railwaymen, including their clerical staff, also solidly backed the strike. Practically all London's bus and tram drivers answered the strike call, though some Underground staff accepted an offer of bonus payments and operated a

A 'black leg' tram is prevented from continuing its journey through the East End by a crowd of demonstrators – some of them showing the clenched-fist Communist salute – during the General Strike of 1926. Food convoys had to be accompanied by armoured cars and troops to avoid hold-ups at strikers' road blocks

skeleton service. Middle-class students, some of them ferried in especially from Oxbridge to 'do their bit' for the government, tried to maintain bus services, though many had to be fenced into their cabs with barbed wire to give them protection from pickets trying to stop them. Still, a number of buses were ambushed by angry crowds who overturned them and set them on fire. Many lorry drivers, however – most of whom were not unionized – continued to work. The main obstacle for them was that men at either end of their journey frequently refused to load or unload their goods.

The Electrical Trade Union solidly backed the strike and voted to close the power stations completely, but the TUC tried to over-rule this and as a result there was confusion – light for home use and power for industry were available in some areas, but there were black-outs in others. In the print industry NATSOPA members – who had, in fact, helped to provoke the final breakdown of negotiations between the government and the unions by refusing to print an anti-union *Daily Mail* editorial – came out strongly in support of the strike. Even the aristocrats of the trade, the Society of Compositors, with 14,000 relatively highly paid members, joined the strike after initially saying they would oppose it. The Fleet Street printing presses were silent for more than a week and although the government produced small quantities of a special emergency newspaper, *The British Gazette*, for the duration of the strike, it had lost an important communication link and means of propaganda in its fight with the unions.

But in a rearguard action the new technology of modern London – over which the government and the well-to-do had considerable control – was marshalled to help defeat the strikers. The BBC transmitted anti-strike radio news broadcasts and speeches by Conservative Prime Minister Stanley Baldwin and other notables, urging the strikers to return to work. The unions were given no access to this new medium.

Tens of thousands of middle-class car owners drove their vehicles to work, offering office workers lifts on the way. In fact, the government had long prepared for this battle with the unions and the motorcar commuter service was part of a whole volunteer system devised to maintain 'business as usual' and keep essential supplies and services going. Although the car service at first caused the biggest traffic jams London had ever seen, this was quickly overcome when the Ministry of Transport set up a massive car park in Horse Guards Parade to which drivers reported for duty. Most of them were surburban housewives. Their journeys could prove quite hazardous, for roving bands of pickets occasionally forced them to abandon their cars and walk home.

Trade union leaders, fearful of provoking a revolution, eventually conceded defeat. This came as a crushing blow to the Labour movement as a whole, but in London it was only a temporary setback. The capital's industrial prosperity helped to sustain strong trade unions and Labour politics, and the Co-operative Movement, which had previously been largely concentrated in the North, continued to flourish in mini-Socialist republics in the London boroughs. Before the 1914-18 War, this sort of radical activity had been so rare in London that it had almost come to be seen as part of an alien Northern culture which could never take root in the South.

Nevertheless, the defeat of the General Strike did dampen the spirit of direct action that was flowering in the poorer parts of London. It was the last major act of popular protest in the capital until the massive anti-Fascist demonstrations of 1936 and the long-running busmen's strike a year later. Legislation was passed to prevent disruptive industrial and political action in the future, and in 1927 all sympathy strikes calculated to coerce the government were banned. Two years later the Local Government Act, passed by the Conservative Government, eliminated any threat of a new wave of Poplarism by disbanding Poor Law Unions and Boards of Guardians. Central government was eager to close any local loopholes through which 'Little Moscows', as they were often called, might emerge. Public Assistance Committees, later superseded by an Unemployment Assistance Board, accountable to central government, were set up, thus making possible a uniform, national policy on unemployment and welfare provision. Although protests and 'overpayments' of benefit continued in some Labour controlled boroughs, for example West Ham, this legislation heralded a new era of centralized control in social services.

A family is evicted by bailiffs under the watchful eye of a policeman at Arch Street, Walworth in 1933. Although standards of living improved for the majority, pockets of absolute poverty and Dickensian slums persisted in inner London throughout the twenties and thirties

Two children peer through the window of a basement flat in East India Dock Road. In 1930 over 100,000 Londoners were living in basement flats that were condemned by Medical Officers of Health as unfit for human habitation – principally because tainted water seeped through their floors and walls every time the sewers beneath them were flooded during heavy rains. These flats provided cosy homes for armies of sewer rats

BUT the shock of these working-class protests in the 1920s gave an added impetus not only to a centralization of power but also to a new wave of poverty investigations. In some ways this interest paralleled the surge of philanthropy and state action which followed the strikes and riots in London in the 1880s and 1890s. Just as in Victorian times social investigators set out to discover the facts about poverty in darkest London, so a new generation ventured into unexplored territory: the old decaying parts of inner London.

This movement really came to fruition in the 1930s. Some donned working-class garb and went to live in the slums of Notting Dale, Soho, Walworth and Stepney, to experience poverty at first hand. To them it was like venturing into darkest Africa – it was a completely different culture from the one they knew – and they drew a harrowing picture of loathsome courts, rat-infested rooms, pawn shops and malnutrition. Joan Conquest condemned the London slums as hotbeds of immorality producing the 'social wreckage' of crime, child battering, illegitimacy and brutalization. And this rediscovery of poverty was taken up by the media in the late 1920s and 30s with BBC radio and leading newspapers making special investigations exposing conditions in London's slumland.

Another big fact-finding mission was begun by two remarkable young men, Charles Madge and Tom Harrisson, who felt that the Press did not accurately record or reflect the experiences of the people themselves. So they launched a project called Mass Observation, setting up one of their main bases at Blackheath. Both had studied anthropology and had what was then the new idea of using an anthropological approach closer to home to capture the minute detail of people's everyday lives. They organized a body of observers, many of them volunteers, to go out into pubs, markets, Labour Exchanges, in fact everywhere, and record what they saw, whom they met and what they said. People were recruited to enter in detail in a diary everything they did on the twelfth day of each month. Thus Madge and Harrisson gathered together an astonishing array of facts. Some of these were published, covering everything from juvenile delinquency, to doing the football pools, to popular jokes, to how many men wore bowler hats in pubs. The observers sometimes went to absurd lengths – which verged on voyeurism – in their pursuit of the facts, as in the following edited report of a man undressing in the East End in February 1939:

Description of male 25, Cockney (Irish) undressing for bed

Time 11.40 to 11.48.40 p.m. Male came into bedroom dressed in blue shirt, dark suit only. He undid the front of his braces and slung them over his shoulder, sat down on bed, immediately got up and lit a cigarette, stood facing bed smoking his cigarette, 20 secs. Talking and motioning with his arms to someone already in bed, 10 secs. Holds his head in his hands, 25 secs. Rolls up his shirt sleeves, picks his nose with his left hand, and rubs it on his shirt. Throws cigarette into fireplace. Motions to person in bed and shows the motions of a boxer, an exhibition lasting 15 secs, pulls off his trousers. Rubs his legs from ankles to knees. Climbs on bed, throws back clothes and slides slowly into bed and pulls clothes over him. Time taken 8 mins 40 secs.

One of the most thorough investigations into poverty in London in fact pre-dated Mass Observation and was completed in 1930 by Llewelyn Smith and his team of researchers from the London School of Economics. They aimed to review the condition of London's poor, forty years after Charles Booth's original poverty survey. Although the report, published in 1934, did record significant improvements in life and labour in London, it documented how half a million people, about one person in eight of the working class, were living below the poverty line. And this wasn't just a definition of poverty appropriate to inter-war consumer London. Llewelyn Smith was using the minimal subsistence definition of poverty which had formed the basis of Charles Booth's 1889 survey of the capital.

The investigation discovered that poverty was concentrated amongst old people, half of whom lived in need because of the meagre pensions of ten shillings a week they were expected to survive on. It was also concentrated amongst widows, single-parent families, families with several children, and the unemployed: these were the people most likely to be living on the bread line. What poverty meant in London in the 1930s was a bread and marge' diet with only occasional meals that included meat; it meant hand-me-down clothes and shoes; and it often meant living in an overcrowded tenement, sharing basic washing, cooking and toilet facilities with other families. Naturally, it inevitably involved an exclusion from most of the modern consumer comforts like an electric iron, a vacuum cleaner and a motor car, that were enjoyed by many middle-class families in London.

Llewellyn Smith's poverty survey was pieced together from a mass of census returns, questionnaires, door-to-door interviews and information obtained from School Attendance Officers, Employment Exchanges and Boards of Guardians. But the nitty gritty of people's actual experiences of poverty are usually drowned in a sea of statistical tables and numerical summaries. Rare glimpses of the scenes his investigators saw appear in a few accounts of interviews with old people, such as Mr N., who eked out an existence on ten shillings a week old age pension, plus six shillings outdoor relief.

Mr N. lives alone in a two-roomed house which is in a very dilapidated condition; most of the paper has come off the walls and the rest is peeling off. The kitchen was very barely furnished and only had a table, a chair and a couch in it, all very dilapidated and almost falling to bits. The room was altogether very miserable and cold, as Mr N. never has a fire until teatime. His clothes were very shabby and needed mending badly. He never got a hot dinner excepting on Sundays; all the rest of the week he has cold meat and bread and cheese. Quite cheerful, he manages to jog along happily and has nothing to worry him and is very contented living alone with his cats. Mr N. goes for a long walk in the park each morning, provided it is not raining and only gets home just in time for dinner. After dinner he cleans up his house and lays the fire and then goes for another walk, coming in just in time for tea. He says that he walks five or six miles every day and feels very fit on it. After tea he sits in front of the fire and reads and smokes. He said that he had great difficulty in getting the Relieving Officer to give him his relief in money; he used to get it in kind as a meat ticket for 3s. 6d. and he said that was of no use to him as he did not want 3s. 6d. worth of meat in a week. He has now got his money and says that he can now save a little in the summer when he has no coals to buy, and with this money he can get things like extra clothes that otherwise he could not get.

Poverty, it was discovered, was widely dispersed around many different parts of inner working-class London. The five poorest areas were Poplar, Bethnal Green, Bermondsey, Stepney and North Kensington, which housed some of the worst in London.

In a few slum streets there was a concentration of poverty, which marked them off as quite beyond the pale of respectable society. These enclaves were marked black on Llewelyn Smith's social map of London. One such street was Campbell Road in North Islington, often described as 'the worst street in North London'. Its tenements were peopled by council labourers, street sellers, the incapacitated – the deaf, the blind, the physically and mentally handicapped – former tramps, the long-term unemployed, prostitutes and small-time crooks. It experienced the most horrendous poverty. There was appalling overcrowding with an average of five people living in each room – as a result two thousand people were jam packed into this small street. A number of houses had no front, back or lavatory doors as these had been chopped up for firewood in hard times. And in the summer many people slept outside in the streets to get some fresh air and to avoid being bitten by the armies of bugs that infested the houses. The residents were in constant and violent conflict with the police over matters like illegal gambling in the streets, prostitution, thieving and drunkenness. When the police intervened they were liable to provoke mini-riots in which virtually the entire street came out to protect their neighbour from arrest.

What all the investigations showed was that the old London, reminiscent of the 1890s, was still there in the 1930s in contrast to the world of cocktails, motor cars and jazz. Although the poverty was usually not so horrendous or so widespread as it had been in Booth's day, there were still dockers out of work, sweat shops paying starvation wages in the East End, muffin men hawking on the streets, and there was still the annual exodus of hop pickers to Kent.

The old sweatshop economy, in which small masters survived the onslaught of factory competition by demanding long hours of labour in return for subsistence wages, trundled on through the 1930s. Blighted by seasonal unemployment, it continued to play an important part in the clothing, boot and shoe, and furniture industries in inner London, especially in the East End. There were still thousands of tiny workshops – usually run by Jewish masters in converted tenements, employing a predominantly Jewish labour force – in the streets of Whitechapel, Bethnal Green and Stepney. London was the last major outpost of this workshop economy in Britain.

There were some glimpses of the twentieth century. A few factories sprang up in the East End, one or two of them responding to the cloth cap craze, which became part of the working-class indentikit in the 1920s and 30s, while others produced cigarettes, catering for the modern fashion of smoking. But many factories migrated to the fringes of London, clustering around the new arterial roads like the Great West Road, the North Circular Road and to a lesser extent Eastern Avenue, where the land was cheaper, and where mass production geared to the needs of the new chain stores like Marks & Spencers and Woolworths was possible. Thus for the most part industry in inner London bore little or no comparison to the modern, Art Deco-style, prosperous factories that were sprouting up in and around the new suburbs.

Where nineteenth-century industry survived in London, it was as a rule associated with the same kind of poverty found in the depressed areas of Britain. London's dockland, for example, had collapsed completely as a commercial venture and had been taken over by the Port of London Authority in 1909. The Authority was formed to try to avert the crippling losses made by many of the old dock companies and to solve the terrible casual labour problem which dragged many dockers and their families down below the poverty line. The building of one of the few major dock extensions of the inter-war years, the King George V Dock at North Woolwich, opened in 1921, was thoroughly in keeping with this image – it was constructed with government funds for the relief of unemployment.

The PLA did help dockers a little through its system of recruiting only from a limited pool of registered dockers, and through its unemployment benefit scheme which assisted those who experienced irregular employment. But still the low wages and the insecurity of unemployment remained. On many occasions, particularly in the slack summer months, there were many more registered men than there was work, with the result that the daily 'call on' at the dock gates sometimes turned into a desperate scramble to be taken by the foreman. The way the new breed of dockers in the 1930s coped with this system – still dominated by the old hook used to grab bags and boxes – is vividly remembered by Alex Gander:

> The hook was important in the life of us dockers. Like the carpenter would have his tools, we'd have our hooks, and when we went to look for work we'd have an S hook in our belt and a bag hook in our pockets. And we'd go on the stones, that was the dockside, or in the 'cage' at the West India Dock, for the call on, to get a day's work. We were like animals in the struggle to get close to the foreman and catch his eye, men would get hooked up to each other. That would lead to aggro, sometimes fights. And you'd get trouble sometimes in the London dock area because a lot of the foremen were Irish and they'd favour their own, so to get around that you'd put a green scarf on so they'd think you were one of them, an R.C.
>
> But the work was irregular and when there wasn't anything doing on the morning call, we'd go to the local coffee shop for a cup of tea and 'two out of the pan', dripping dipped in the pan. Then it was on to the local police courts to see the drunks and the prostitutes and petty thieves, then on to the library to read.
>
> We'd look at Lloyds to see when and where the boats were coming in, and if there were some due in at Tilbury, we'd go down there on spec' to look for work. Usually, though, we'd stay around for the afternoon call, and if there wasn't any work then we'd go to the billiard hall or go home. If you had three consecutive days in a week without any work you got some dole money. So if we'd had two days off we weren't very keen to work on the third because you ended up losing money. And if we worked three days and the other three were on the dole, we had a saying, we'd call it 'three on the hook and three on the book' or 'the bomper'.

The rediscovery of this sort of hardship and poverty in the inter-war years went hand in hand with a renewed attempt to do something about it. Charitable and voluntary work, initiated through a complex web of care committees, housing trusts, settlement missions, and so on, was given a new

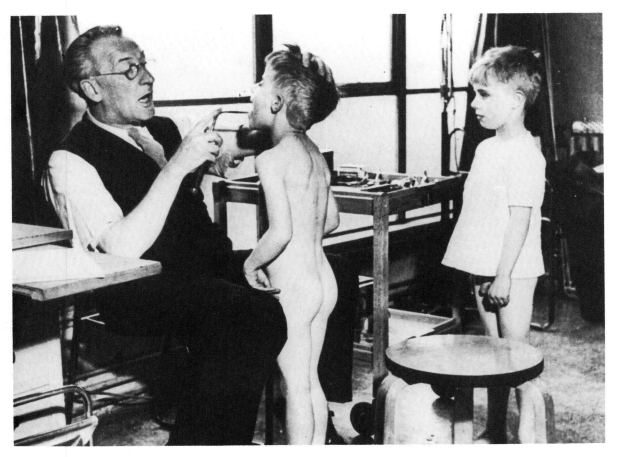

sense of urgency. One pioneering voluntary project in London at this time was the launching of the Peckham Health Centre. Two radical doctors – George Scott Williamson and Innes Pearse – first established an experimental centre in a small house in London's declining mid-Victorian suburb in 1926, the aim being to monitor and devise ways of maintaining health and preventing illness in the local community – preventative medicine was then quite a novel idea. The centre was later closed down for a few years while a massive effort was made to raise enough money to construct a new purpose-built home. It opened again in 1935 in a modern, open-plan building which boasted a swimming pool, a gymnasium and a cafeteria. The centre sought to create an attractive meeting-place where all the family could be together – only whole families were allowed to join – and which would integrate exercise, sport, health care and check-ups into the everyday life of the local community.

But the most successful attempt to build a 'New Jerusalem' in a run-down part of London was in Bermondsey. Here a radical Socialist and philanthropist, Dr Alfred Salter, joined forces with working-class Labour councillors to create a miniature welfare state, incorporating the latest medical equipment. In 1926 the Labour Council opened a 'Sun Cure Institute', the first municipal solarium in Britain. Sun treatment helped to cure and keep

'Say ah'. Twins are given a check-up at the Peckham Health Centre in the late thirties. The centre pioneered new approaches in family-based preventative medicine – part of an inter-war movement to improve the people's health

Following page, above: A solarium in the Bermondsey Health Centre in the 1930s. Goggled local children, suffering from T.B. and rickets, are treated with the artificial sunlight of the sun ray lamp. Bermondsey boasted the first solarium in Britain

Below: Bermondsey children at Leysin, Switzerland, in 1930. The Council paid for severe T.B. cases to be sent to a special school where they enjoyed a two-year fresh air and sunshine treatment in the Swiss Alps

at bay tuberculosis, which flourished in Bermondsey's environment of malnutrition, overcrowding and bad air. A year later one of the most magnificent baths in the country was opened, which included two swimming pools, 126 private baths, and Turkish and Russian vapour baths. This was a

The *Bermondsey Labour Magazine*, September 1926, proudly extolling the local Labour Council's efforts to beautify Bermondsey and bring the country into London

Please pay the Steward for your copy, or send Annual Subscription to the Editor, 57, Upper Grange Road, S.E.1. Every penny paid helps to ensure the regular publication of the Magazine month by month. Where the copies are not paid for, the stewards are instructed to leave a free copy. PLEASE PAY IF YOU CAN.

BERMONDSEY LABOUR MAGAZINE

No. 32.   Editor : J. A. W. Douglas.   September, 1926.   Price 1d.

The Official Organ of the   *Bermondsey Labour Movement.*

Beautifying Bermondsey

An army of sunbathers and swimmers descend on George Lansbury's Lido in Hyde Park during the summer of 1937. Lidos were part of the thirties' cult of fresh air, keep fit and sunshine

badly needed amenity because only one home in a hundred had a bath in Bermondsey. But the pinnacle of the Labour Council's achievements came with the creation of a purpose-built, modern health centre in 1936 – they saw it as the Harley Street of Bermondsey – which rehoused the solarium and boasted amongst its many departments a foot clinic, a clinic for ear, nose, throat and eye ailments, an ante-natal clinic, and a dental surgery. As a result of their efforts, the death rate and the infant mortality rate both fell dramatically in Bermondsey between the wars.

This kind of social reform was given much wider currency and was heavily promoted when the London Labour Party under Herbert Morrison gained control of the LCC in 1934. Labour got into power on a rising tide of concern – particularly amongst the middle classes – that local authorities should take a more active role in tackling the social problems of the capital. Morrison's vision of municipal socialism was different from that of George Lansbury and the rebellious Poplar councillors in the early twenties. The latter had used the language of class war and favoured direct action: if necessary, they did not hesitate to break the law. What Morrison offered was a more moderate programme of change, planning by professionals, and improvements in housing and public services to be voted in through the ballot box. It was a package designed to attract not just working-class voters, but also middle-class voters with a social conscience.

He recruited sympathetic advertisement agency men and women to streamline his party's image and give it a vigorous and progressive look. They came up with slogans like 'Let Labour Build the New London', 'Labour Gets Things Done', 'A Healthy London', 'A Decent Treatment for the Poor', and 'For The Children's Sake'. This formula won Labour control of the LCC from 1934 to 1940, and during these years new directives from County Hall further changed the face of the capital. This was the era of a Morrison-style 'brave new world' for Londoners: the heyday, in a way, of the LCC which had much wider responsibilities in those pre-welfare state days.

The party quickly drew up three-year programmes for housing, health, education, town planning and parks. Most effort was put into housing, and hundreds of blocks of modern council flats rose out of the rubble of the worst slums, which the LCC bought through compulsory purchase orders in places like Camberwell, Lambeth and Poplar. The LCC also began to refashion the workhouse hospitals it took over from the Boards of Guardians in 1929. Under the new Morrison regime hospitals were modernized and re-equipped, sun balconies were built, more staff was recruited, diets were improved, and wirelesses were installed for patients. In the field of education, what were termed the 'Tory Shylockisms' – the economy cuts – were abolished, staffing levels were increased, free milk supplied, and health inspections provided. School prizes were restored, more scholarships to secondary schools introduced, and children in residential schools were given a camp holiday every summer.

Morrison's municipal socialism was channelled into improving and increasing the number of parks, playing fields and open spaces: a change very much inspired by the thirties' enthusiasm for fresh air, healthy exercise,

Free milk for children in the London parks during the school summer holidays of 1937. It was provided by the LCC as part of their campaign to improve the health of poorer children and to keep them off the streets of London

A voluntary 'Care Committee' worker visits a poor family in Hoxton in 1939. A resurgence of this sort of charitable work was one feature of the mainly council-led, inter-war social reform movement

sunbathing and sport. Many parks, like Victoria Park in Hackney, were provided with more facilities such as paddling pools, modern lidos with purified water, sun-bathing terraces, cafés, bowling greens, and tennis courts. Morrison was particularly proud of the amenities for open-air entertainment that were provided during school holidays, when comedians, conjurors and story-tellers attracted big crowds of children in the parks. By 1938 the LCC provided 347 cricket pitches, 436 football pitches (of which 140 were on Hackney Marshes), and 713 tennis courts.

Morrison's most controversial act was the rebuilding of Waterloo Bridge. The old bridge, dating from 1817 and opened on the anniversary of the Battle of Waterloo, had been in poor condition since the 1920s, but Parliament was reluctant to demolish it, or to contribute to the cost of a new bridge. There was great conservation pressure to save the old bridge, which was regarded as an architectural masterpiece. However, when he came to power, Morrison set in motion a rebuilding programme: he wanted a functional bridge which would carry LCC trams. The new Waterloo Bridge should have been completed by 1940: in fact it had to wait until 1945 as the war delayed construction. But the rebuilding was regarded as a great symbolic triumph of the LCC over central government and of socialist pragmatism over reactionary conservation.

By the time Morrison came to power, the continuing expansion of London was beginning to become a political issue, and it was he who began a scheme for limiting its growth. This was the beginning of a 'green belt' policy, to ring the capital with fields and parkland protected from further suburban development, mentioned in Chapter Four. It was an expression of the ideal of city life which, in a sense, epitomized the belief in planning for a new, cleaner, healthier world.

There is no doubt that municipal reform in the inter-war years achieved a great deal: it was a kind of prototype welfare state run at a local, rather than a national level. But there were inevitably limits to what it could accomplish, and then, as now, central government was watchful and jealous of the power local authorities could wield. The actions of the Poplar councillors in flouting the conventional administration of the old Poor Law, for example, and similar subsequent protests elsewhere, were taken as reasons for the gradual dismantling of this Victorian system of welfare from 1929 onwards. Power was progressively removed from local guardians, and from the Public Assistance Boards which replaced them, as a more standardized, nationally-controlled system replaced the variable local administration. Though Poor Law Guardians were rarely generous, the Assistance Board inspectors enforced a 'social security' administration quite heartless by later standards.

Despite the fact that London was very prosperous compared with the rest of Britain in the 1930s, some districts, such as Poplar and Stepney, suffered severe unemployment, rising to fifteen or even twenty per cent. Poverty-striken families in such areas had now to pass the 'means test' if they were to get public assistance – the income of the whole family, including children, and their possessions were scrutinized and totted up before they were eligible for help. Inspectors could go into any claimant's home, demand that anything deemed a 'luxury' – such as the radio or gramophone – be sold, and the proceeds would be docked from benefit payments.

There was nothing the idealistic municipal Socialists could do about this, and while they might provide solariums and parks for poorer Londoners, more fundamental economic need persisted. In this climate, the unemployed remained a potentially aggressive and perhaps revolutionary force, whose sympathies could be sought by the Communist Party, or by the Communist-controlled National Unemployed Workers movement, which staged many of the hunger marches on the capital, as well as one or two sensational publicity stunts in London itself. In the nineteenth century, there had been riots in the West End: in the 1930s, groups of penniless, unemployed workers invaded the Ritz and asked to be fed, as Chris Cansick, a revolutionary diner of the period, can recall:

> There was about fourteen of us, and we'd decided, 'We're gonna have dinner at the Ritz'. So we went in smartly, walked to the table, sat down, we had our working clothes on, the only clothes we had, you know. The waiter come up, 'Gentlemen what do you want, what are you here for?'
>
> 'We would like a dinner please'.
>
> 'Dinner! Dinner!'
>
> He said it so many times, so we said 'Yes'.
>
> 'I'll get the manager'.
>
> So he got the manager. Now they didn't want trouble, the Ritz, because the unemployed were there and the unemployed could wreck the place,

that's what they thought. So the manager got onto the police and they were waiting outside, but we still said, 'We're not going, we're going to stop here till we have something to eat'.

I was really afraid, I said to myself, 'this is it'. Anyway, they didn't call the police in, they didn't want it in the papers, 'the unemployed at the Ritz', bad publicity, the big nobs go to the Ritz. So some dinners came up, always remember it, meat and potatoes we had, and sweet afterwards, and tea. We thoroughly enjoyed it.

So we got up after the meal, we was on pins and needles, we were saying, 'That's our lot, "Pentonville now".'

'No, sod Pentonville' old Sid said, 'We'll do it on our knees'.

Anyway, we marched out, and the police didn't touch us, and there was a van drawn up outside, full of our mates, and they gave us all these bills and banners they'd just made, and we marched all around Piccadilly, saying it was the finest meal we'd ever had. That was a great day for the unemployed.

A much more serious threat to the peaceful, gradualist mainstream of social reform in the capital was the emergence in the 1930s of pockets of strong support for the Communist Party on the one hand, and for the British Union of Fascists on the other. Both represented essentially European, radical approaches to solving the problems of poverty and inequality; the key ideological battleground at the time was in Spain where, during the Civil War, the entire nation was divided by these competing political philosophies.

In London, though neither Sir Oswald Mosley's followers – the Blackshirts – nor the Communists ever commanded more than local and limited support, the East End did for a time become a battleground. This part of the capital, traditionally the first port of call of immigrants arriving by ship from the Continent, had always had a European flavour. Since the 1880s, with the arrival of large numbers of immigrants escaping pogroms in Russia and elsewhere in Eastern Europe, it had supported a sizeable Jewish community. Even before the First World War, the European Jewish anarchist had been a recognizable figure in the East End: now, in the 1930s, quite a number of Jews embraced Communism.

They were encouraged to do so by the Fascists, who made the Jews political scapegoats, as was happening in Nazi Germany. Though the Fascists' anti-semitism was not generally endorsed in the national newspapers, their political policies were given considerable backing by the *Daily Mail*, the *Evening News* and the *Sunday Despatch*. For the Jews of the East End, the Blackshirts represented a physical threat: the windows of Jewish shops were smashed and Blackshirts marched through the streets chanting anti-semitic slogans.

The Communist Party presented the most immediate and vociferous opposition to this bullying, and many young Jews joined, prepared to fight back. In 1936 the conflict came to a head, after many skirmishes in London, in what became known as the Battle of Cable Street.

When the Fascists organized a march through a Jewish quarter of the East End, the Labour Party advised opponents to stay at home. The Communist

Party, however, adopted a policy of direct opposition on the streets and organized a counter-demonstration of about 100,000 supporters, a great many of them Jewish. Barricades were thrown across the streets by the Communist opposition, and many fights broke out, including a flare-up in Cable Street in Bethnal Green before the march was finally abandoned.

In broad political terms, the Cable Street incident was not of lasting significance, except in the sense that it provided ammunition for reformers such as Morrison to argue the case for social change which might remove the underlying causes of discontent. And it was quickly overshadowed by the threat of war in Europe which by 1938 was being taken seriously. The reformist movement, which had attempted to improve the lives of the poor

A Communist barricade about to be dismantled by the police during the Cable Street riots of October 1936. During the thirties the East End, with its large Jewish community, became a battleground for Fascists and Communists

through a healthier environment was now complemented by a national concern about the health of a people who would need strength to fight a war with Germany. Schemes like the National Fitness Campaign, launched in 1938, encouraged the provision of more recreational facilities.

London was now regarded in quite a new light. Until the Green Belt policy of 1935, almost nothing had been done to prevent its continued growth and the social problems thereby created. Now it appeared to those who might have to fight a modern war that it had become an enormous and absurd liability, into which the lion's share of the nation's wealth had been poured in the twenties and thirties. The terrible damage that could be inflicted by air attack – regarded as insignificant in the First World War – had been demonstrated in the Spanish Civil War. And here was London, a metropolis of more than eight million people, within easy striking distance of the enemy.

In 1938 the Committee on Imperial Defence estimated that in the first twenty-four hours of war, 175,000 Londoners would be killed, and the toll would rise to 1,800,000 after two months. There were plans for mass war graves, as someone had calculated that 20 million square feet of timber would be needed if the dead were all buried in coffins. Winston Churchill commented that London was 'the greatest target in the world, a kind of tremendous, fat, valuable cow, fed up to attract beasts of prey'.

So London's great strength in economic terms during the inter-war period had by 1938 become a liability. And though the horrifying prophesies of the effects of air raids were never fulfilled, the realization that the capital had become dangerously bloated put an end to its uncontrolled expansion. During the Second World War, government departments were despatched to the provinces, and in the reconstruction of the 1940s and 1950s government policy was to reduce the dominance of the capital and to control its expansion. In the administration of the health and welfare services of the capital, the essentially local municipalism of the 1930s was to be superseded by much greater state provision.

The sense that an era in London's history was coming to an end in 1938 – a period in which its Victorian culture and structure had been replaced by a brave new world of council housing, mock-Tudor suburbia, sun-bathing by the Serpentine, American jazz, electricity and the motor car – was expressed in an extraordinary outburst of nostalgia.

In that year, a song and dance routine, *The Lambeth Walk*, was performed by Lupino Lane in the West End show 'Me and My Girl'. The words of the song conjured up a sentimental image of the old London of community spirit in a Victorian back street, while the dance routine involved much marching up and down, head waving, and the shouting of 'Oi' as the hand, thumb cocked, was swung in an over-the-shoulder gesture.

It was such a success, both nationally and internationally – Mussolini is said to have ordered a pretty girl to teach it to him in Italy – that the archetypal thirties social scientific reform group, Mass Observation, made a study of it. They could not really explain the phenomenon, except in terms of a harking back to the old days – a kind of wild rejection of the new – and marvelled at the scenes it brought to London, where dancing had been a great inter-war craze. One Mass Observation report stated:

At Highbury Fields, Islington, on August 11 (1938) the crowds totalled some 20,000 and the official arrangements broke down under the strain. The inner ring of asphalt meant for the dancers became lined on both sides with onlookers as well, leaving only a narrow lane for dancing. One had to fight to get in or out of this ring. Announcements and speeches were drowned by the voice of the crowd in spite of powerful loudspeakers. The Lambeth Walk was the chief excitement, though the dancers in the end just tramped and bombed around in a solid mass, speeding into a blind scrum.

It is difficult now to conjure up such extraordinary scenes, just as it is hard to recapture the degree to which London between the wars was so very different from the Victorian capital, and yet quite remote from the place we know today. The faith and conviction of reformers who believed that in great council blocks they were building a Utopian society of the future; who thought modern science would solve the problems of the nation and the capital; and who set out to create a brave new world seem now to be simply quaint, outmoded and naive. It has been said of the thirties as an historical period that the years passed straight from history into myth, and to bring them into clear focus is not easy.

In this book, and the television series it accompanies, we hope we have brought back, and provided some explanation of, the reality of the years between the Zeppelin raids of the Great War, and the period when Londoners went home to their semi-detached retreats with gas masks to await a second holocaust.

Inset: Doing the Lambeth Walk in Whitechapel in 1938. This song and dance craze, which emerged from the West End show 'Me and My Girl', provided Britain with its biggest international hit in the new jazz age

Above: Doing the Lambeth Walk at the Savoy Hotel, 1939: the craze gripped all classes of society. It conjured up a reassuring and nostalgic image of old London peopled with chirpy Cockneys, as Britain lurched towards another world war

FURTHER READING

Of the many books we have read, the following were particularly interesting and informative. We found the most readable, and colourful, books providing a survey of inter-war Britain to be Noreen Branson, *Britain in the Nineteen Twenties* (Weidenfeld & Nicolson, 1975) and Noreen Branson and Margot Heinemann, *Britain in the Nineteen Thirties* (Weidenfeld & Nicolson, 1971). Also, Llewellyn Smith, *The New Survey of London Life and Labour* – 9 vols (P.S. King, 1930) is a mine of information on many aspects of inter-war London, comparing and contrasting it with the London of Charles Booth's 1889 survey.

Books which contain useful material on the 'invasion' of London, and on social, economic and architectural changes in the capital during the inter-war years are: H. Castle, *Fire over England: German Air Raids in World War, A History* (Secker & Warburg, 1983); Arthur Marwick, *The Deluge: British Society and The First World War* (Macmillan, 1965); Leslie Hannah, *The Rise of the Corporate Economy* (Methuen, 1983); Christopher Bigsby (ed.), *American Popular Culture and Europe* (Elek, 1975); Hermione Hobhouse, *A History of Regent Street* (Macdonald & Janes, 1975); and the Survey of London, especially vol. 39 (1977), vol. 40 (1980), and vol. 41 (1983) – all published by the GLC.

For the Empire to Electricity chapter, we found interesting information in Brian Bowers, *A History of Electric Light and Power* (Peter Peregrinus, 1982), Leslie Hannah, *Electricity Before Nationalisation* (Macmillan, 1979), Peter Hall, *The Industries of London Since 1861* (Hutchinson, 1962), D.H. Smith, *The Industries of London* (P.S. King, 1933), Geoffrey Hewlett (ed.), *A History of Wembley* (London Borough of Brent, 1979) and James Morris, *Farewell the Trumpets: An Imperial Retreat* (Penguin, 1981).

On transport, the most informative books are Alan Jackson, *Rails Through the Clay: A History of London's Tube Railways* (Allen & Unwin, 1962), T. Barker and M. Robbins, *A History of London Transport Vol. 2: The Twentieth Century* (Allen & Unwin, 1974), Christian Barman, *The Man who Built London Transport: A Biography of Frank Pick* (David & Charles, 1979), William Plowden, *The Motor Car and Politics, 1896-1970* (Bodley Head, 1971), Colin Buchanan, *Mixed Blessings: The Motor in Britain* (Leonard Hill, 1958) and Oliver Green and John Reed, *The London Transport Golden Jubilee Book* (Daily Telegraph, 1983).

We found the most interesting works on London's inter-war suburban development to be: Alan Jackson, *Semi-Detached London: Suburban Development, Life and Transport 1900-39* (Allen & Unwin, 1973); Ken Young and Patricia Garside, *Metropolitan London: Politics and Urban Change 1837-1981* (Edward Arnold, 1982); and M. Carr, 'The Development and Character of a Metropolitan Suburb: Bexley, Kent' in F.M.L. Thompson, *The Rise of Suburbia* (Leicester University Press, 1982). Also useful for the immediate post-war years is Mark Swenarton, *Homes Fit for Heroes* (Heinemann, 1981), and for a more general account, John Burnett, *A Social History of Housing 1815-1970* (David & Charles, 1978). Especially interesting contemporary analyses of the new cottage estates are Ruth Durant, *Watling: A Survey of Social Life on a New Housing Estate* (P.S. King, 1939) and Terence Young, *Becontree and Dagenham* (Samuel Siddars, 1934). For the story of the plotlanders, see Dennis Hardey and Colin Ward, *Arcadia For All: The Legacy of a Makeshift Landscape* (Mansell, 1984).

For interesting and informative studies on 'ideal homes', the servantless house and life in the new suburbs, see Paul Oliver *et al*, *Dunroamin: The Suburban Semi and Its Enemies* (Barrie & Jenkins, 1981), Alan Jackson, see above, Adrian Forty, 'The Electric Home: A Case Study of the Domestic Revolution of the inter-war years' in *Open University*, History of Architecture and Design Course, *British Design* (Units 19.20, 1980), J. Richards, *Castles on the Ground* (Architectural Press, 1946), and Mark Swenarton, 'Having a Bath. English Domestic Bathrooms, 1890-1940' in *Leisure in the Twentieth Century* (Design Council, 1976). For provocative arguments on the position of women and their role as housewife during the inter-war years, see Jane Lewis, 'Women Between the Wars' in Frank Gleversmith (ed.) *Class, Culture and Social Change: A New View of the 1930s* (Harvester Press, 1983) and Di Gittins, *The Fair Sex: Family Size and Structure 1900-39* (Hutchinson, 1982). We found the most useful social and architectural histories of the British cinema to be Dennis Sharp, *The Picture Palace* (Hugh Evelyn, 1969) and D. Atwell, *Cathedrals of the Movies: History of the British Cinema and their Audiences* (Architectural Press, 1981).

The best histories of post-war London Labour Party idealism are Noreen Branson, *Poplarism 1919-1925: George Lansbury and the Councillors' Revolt* (Lawrence & Wishart, 1979) and Fenner Brockway, *Bermondsey Story* (Bermondsey Independent Labour Party, 1949). Also useful for the brave new world ethos and the rediscovery of poverty are: Bernard Donoughue and G.W. Jones, *Herbert Morrison: Portrait of a Politician* (Weidenfeld & Nicholson, 1973); Tim Benton, 'The Biologist's Lens – The Pioneer Health Centre' in *Architectural Design, Britain in the Thirties* (1979); Angus Calder and Dorothy Sheridan, *Speak for Yourself: A Mass Observation Anthology 1937-49* (Jonathan Cape, 1984); and *The New Survey of London Life and Labour* see above, especially vol. III.

INDEX

THE MAKING OF MODERN LONDON 1815-1914

Gavin Weightman & Steve Humphries

London is essentially a modern city, despite the 'olde worlde' image projected to tourists. In the years between the Battle of Waterloo and the outbreak of the First World War, London grew and developed into the first great metropolis of the industrial age, the heart not only of a thriving nation but also of a great colonial empire.

The authors plot the transformation of the City from a merchants' stronghold into the world's leading financial centre. They trace the way in which 'Society' with its 'Season' laid the foundations for the immense growth of the West End, pushing westwards into the countryside and developing areas like Kensington and Notting Hill. They show how the fate of the East End was to be quite different: the building of the docks, the development of sweated industries and massive immigration transformed this rural, seafaring community into a vast expanse of mean streets which came to symbolize the terrible poverty of imperial London. Finally, they look at the making of the suburbs: the early, clerkish areas of Hackney, Islington and Camberwell; and the later growth, aided and abetted by the horse and the railway, of such suburbs as Ealing, Clapham and Brixton.

Today we are familiar with great cities with several million inhabitants – the suburb, the commuter railway, docklands and decaying city centres are commonplace features. But what makes London unique, and so fascinating to explore, is that all these elements were present over a century ago, producing the largest and most complex urban development the world had ever known.

'As a brief and evocative introduction to the world city at its zenith, this book is warmly to be recommended. The authors are well up on recent monographs on the subject; the themes are well chosen and articulated; and the illustrations are a delight.'

David Cannadine, **Sunday Times**

'**The Making of Modern London** is about a subject strangely neglected, packing in more surprises than can be easily digested in one reading.' Alan Brien, **The Guardian**